Kentu

Hearts are racing and all bets are off!

Cousins Callee Dobson and Christina Mobbs are both dedicated to their patients. Callee to all the people at Churchill Downs, home of the Kentucky Derby, and Christina to her animals, including an equine contender for the derby who needs her care. These feisty Southern belles have both had their fair share of heartache, so it's easy for them to throw themselves into their work. Until trauma doc Langston Watts and Irish veterinarian Conor O'Brian arrive to give them a run for their money and put their hearts on the line...

Join Susan Carlisle's Kentucky Derby Medics as they buckle up for the greatest race of all—the final furlong to their happy-ever-afters in

Callee and Langston's story, *Falling for the Trauma Doc*

Christina and Conor's story, *An Irish Vet in Kentucky*

Both available now!

Dear Reader,

It's with great pleasure that I wrote this book. I have attended the Kentucky Derby and enjoyed it so much that I wanted to share those moments with you. The fact I had the opportunity to revisit that exciting time was fun. I hope you enjoy Christina and Conor's love story against the backdrop of Churchill Downs and the greatest two minutes in sports.

I love to hear from my readers. Please contact me at susan.carlisle@ymail.com.

Happy reading,

Susan

AN IRISH VET IN KENTUCKY

SUSAN CARLISLE

Harlequin

MEDICAL ROMANCE

Harlequin®
MEDICAL ROMANCE

ISBN-13: 978-1-335-94261-6

An Irish Vet in Kentucky

Copyright © 2024 by Susan Carlisle

Harlequin Enterprises ULC
22 Adelaide St. West, 41st Floor
Toronto, Ontario M5H 4E3, Canada
www.Harlequin.com

Printed in U.S.A.

Recycling programs for this product may not exist in your area.

Susan Carlisle's love affair with books began when she made a bad grade in mathematics. Not allowed to watch TV until the grade had improved, she filled her time with books. Turning her love of reading into a love for writing romance, she pens hot medicals. She loves castles, traveling, afternoon tea, reading voraciously and hearing from her readers. Join her newsletter at susancarlisle.com.

Books by Susan Carlisle

Harlequin Medical Romance

Atlanta Children's Hospital

Mending the ER Doc's Heart
Reunited with the Children's Doc
Wedding Date with Her Best Friend
Second Chance for the Heart Doctor

Kentucky Derby Medics

Falling for the Trauma Doc

Pacific Paradise, Second Chance
The Single Dad's Holiday Wish
Reunited with Her Daredevil Doc
Taming the Hot-Shot Doc
From Florida Fling to Forever

Visit the Author Profile page
at Harlequin.com for more titles.

To Thomas

I'll love you forever.

CHAPTER ONE

CONOR O'BRIAN STEPPED into the dim stable hall to a view of a female behind encased in dusty jeans, raised in the air and swinging back and forth. For the first time in a long time, he took a moment to admire the well-developed lines of a woman's firm bottom.

He cleared his throat to gain her attention and adjusted his focus. "Excuse me, but I'm looking for the owner."

The woman straightened then shoved the pitchfork she held into a pile of loose hay. With a swift practiced move, she flipped it off the fork over a stall wall. Dust floated around her in the stream of light coming in through the doors.

"Hello," he said louder.

She whirled, making her rust-colored ponytail whip round her head, the pitchfork held like a weapon. With a slim build, the plaid shirt, jeans and boots covered the curves he'd admired earlier. What caught his attention was the sparkle in her brilliant green eyes. Ones that reminded him of the countryside at home after a rain.

"Ho. Ho." He threw up his hands and stepped back. She stood almost as tall as he did. "I'm just looking for the person who owns the stables."

"What?" She leaned the handle of the pitchfork against the wall then pulled white speaker buds from her ears. "Can I help you?"

"I'm looking for the owner." How long was this non-conversation going to go on? He was tired, having traveled all day.

She placed her hands on her hips and glared at him. "You found her."

His step faltered. This woman he hadn't anticipated. She looked more like a farmhand than the veterinarian he had been told she was. "I'm Conor O'Brian. I understood you would be expecting me."

Her eyes narrowed and her brow wrinkled. In a sweet Southern drawl she said, "I'm sorry. I don't recognize that name."

Had he been sent on a wild-goose chase? He had no desire to make this trip to begin with, but William Guinness, Liquid Gold's owner, had insisted Conor come with the horse. Someone who knew the animal well enough to see about him in the weeks leading up to the Kentucky Derby. Conor's siblings had encouraged him to make the trip as well. Now this.

"I was told that Gold would be stabled here for two weeks before moving to the racetrack barns."

The woman's face brightened. Her body relaxed. "Liquid Gold. Yes, the horse from Ireland. I wasn't expecting him until day after tomorrow. I should've guessed from your accent who you might be." At least she had expected the horse if not him.

She stepped forward and offered her hand. "I'm Christina Mobbs. Welcome to Seven Miles Farm and Stables."

He liked the name *Christina.* But they were not friends, so he settled on calling her by a more formal name. "Dr. Mobbs, I would really like to get Gold settled. It's been a long trip. The flight, then three days in quarantine in Indianapolis, then the three-hour drive here. I think he needs something stable under his feet."

"Certainly. I have a stall ready." She walked farther down the hall and opened a stall door wide, then returned to him and moved beyond.

Conor stepped outside just behind her. He glanced at the countryside. It reminded him of home with its green trees and grass-covered rolling hills. At least that much he could appreciate about being here. Except he'd rather be in Ireland in his own home, being left alone.

Conor had pushed back about coming here but the knowledge that his brother and sister were worried about him had made him agree. They feared he had become too insulated and removed from life because of his loneliness and anger over losing Louisa and his unborn child. They had said they even feared for his mental health. Their idea was that with a change of scenery he might snap out of his depression. He didn't share the idea that a trip to the United States would change his mindset, but he had been left with little choice but to make the trip. After all, it was only for three weeks. What could happen in that amount of time?

Christina put out a hand as if to touch the large white truck and kept it there as she walked beside the matching horse trailer. "Nice rig."

"Not my doing but I agree it is nice."

"I'm going to need to see some papers before I let you unload him. Do you have a health certificate, import permit and blood tests?"

"I have them right here." He handed her the papers he had pulled out of his back pocket.

She flipped through the sheets, running a finger down each page. "Looks good. The training and racing certificates are even here." She handed them back to him and continued to the rear of the trailer.

Conor joined her there. Inside, he could hear Gold shifting his weight, making the trailer creak. After opening the back door wide, he pulled the ramp out and stepped inside. "Easy, boy. We're done traveling for a while. It's time to rest and get ready for the big day." Conor spoke softly, running his hand across the Thoroughbred's neck. "You have a nice stall waiting. Just for you."

Only with his equine patients had Conor felt like himself since his wife had killed herself and their unborn baby. Working with the horses eased his pain, or at least let him forget for a few minutes. With the horses, he dared to care.

"Let's get you out of here." He untied the halter rope from the bar in the trailer. Turning Gold, Conor led him out and down the metal ramp. He looked at Dr. Mobbs, who stood beside the driver, to see a look of pure pleasure on her face.

"What a fine-looking horse." Awe hung in each of her words.

"He is a handsome fellow. And fast, too." Conor could not help but speak like a proud parent. "I've been taking care of him since his birth."

"I would like to examine him before you put him in the stall." She stepped toward them.

"Why?"

She looked directly at him. "Because this is my place and if something is wrong with such an expensive piece of horseflesh, I want to know about it. I'm a veterinarian. I know what I'm doing. I also need to know Gold isn't carrying anything that might make the other horses here ill."

Conor straightened his shoulders. He wasn't used to anyone questioning his care of Gold or any other animal for that matter. "I assure you Gold is in fine health."

"Still, I must insist if he is to stay at Seven Miles."

She walked to the front of the horse, lifting his head with a hand under the horse's chin. "You are indeed a handsome fellow."

Conor watched as Christina looked into Gold's eyes, pulled up his lips to study his teeth and then ran her hand over his shoulders and back before doing the same to his legs.

She had a gentle but firm touch. Gold didn't take to just anyone; that was part of why William had wanted Conor with Gold, but the horse seemed content with Christina's attention. Did she have that effect on all males she touched? He pushed away that uncomfortable idea. What had made such a foreign thought flash through his mind? He hadn't thought of a woman that way since his wife died. Hadn't wanted to.

"I understand he was the highest point earner in the Europe seven-race circuit." She continued around to the other side of the horse.

"That is correct. That's why he was issued an invitation to the Derby race."

"You know no visiting horse has ever won

the Derby." She looked at him from under the horse's neck.

Conor shrugged. "There is always a first time."

She grinned, taking his breath for a moment.

Christina had to admit the horse was in prime condition. Not unlike the man assigned to handle Gold, despite a sadness that shrouded him. It particularly showed in his blue eyes that held a hollow, haunted look. She had instated a look-but-don't-touch program after her no-good ex, Nelson had pulled his trick last year. After that horrible experience she didn't allow herself to trust anyone. She had considered herself a good judge of character until she'd been proven wrong in a very painful way.

When she stepped away from the horse, the Irish man said, "Now it's my turn."

She watched as wide, confident fingers repeated what she had just finished.

The horse's muscles rippled beneath his administrations. The animal stood still, obviously used to the man's hands.

All the while Conor spoke in a soft, low voice. His deep Irish baritone washed over her.

It made her think of the warmth of a fire on a cold, snowy night, pushing all the drafts away.

She hadn't had that in her life for too long.

What did she have to do to keep him talking so she could bask in that feeling just a little longer?

Instead of finding an answer to her internal question, she stood there looking at him as if she'd never seen a handsome man before. Shaking herself figuratively, she redirected herself to the thoughtfulness he gave the horse's legs. He spent more time on them than he had other areas of the animal's body, giving them a thorough assessment. She watched, mesmerized. It always amazed her how so much weight and strength could rest on such thin supports. A racehorse full-out running was pure majesty.

Once again, Christina's consideration fell to the man doing the exam. The thick, dark waves on his head captured her interest.

A tense, blue-eyed look snagged hers, held. "He fared well for such a long trip."

"I would agree." She managed not to stammer.

The man squatted beside the horse. He reminded her of a Thoroughbred, slim and moving with slick, easy motions.

The driver of the truck stated he had to go if he was no longer needed. Conor removed his bag from the backseat and shook the man's hand. Minutes later they watched the truck and trailer rattle down the drive.

"Let's get Gold in his stall." She turned and entered the barn.

He followed with Gold on a lead.

A half an hour later they had Gold settled in a stall.

Conor stepped back from the stall gate. "It's always tough on a horse when it travels."

"Yes, and horses that are good enough to run the Kentucky Derby tend to be rather high-strung."

"Exactly. That's why Mr. Guinness's trainer wanted Gold to come a few weeks early. It gives him a chance to settle in. He can spend the time acclimating to the weather. Kentucky's humidity alone is far different from Ireland's."

"I imagine it is." One day she would love the chance to visit Ireland.

Conor continued, "I, on the other hand, am worn out. Could you show me where I will be staying? It's been a long day and the time change still has me out of sync."

Her head shifted to the side. What was he talking about? Her mouth twisted in thought. Dr. Dillard, the head veterinarian of the clinic at Churchill Downs, had said nothing about someone staying at her farm. She boarded and cared for horses. Not men she didn't know. "Uh… You're expecting to stay here?"

"Yes, I understood I would be staying near Gold." He looked around. "It doesn't look like there is a hotel on every corner, so I assume I'm to stay in the house."

"That isn't what I understood." But Dr. Dillard might have failed to tell her.

"I'm afraid that isn't going to work. I don't know you and it's just me here. I wasn't expecting to board you as well."

Dr. Dillard had asked if she would be willing to board Gold for two weeks. She needed the money and the doctor's goodwill since she wanted to work the Derby week at Churchill Downs. After what Nelson had done to her, she needed to prove to her peers she was nothing like Nelson and wasn't involved in his drug selling. The Derby only took the best veterinarians, and she wanted that seal of approval. She'd been working for the invitation to serve all year long.

"I will pay you twice what a hotel would charge me. Make it three times."

"You really want to stay here."

"Gold is my responsibility. I take that seriously. I need to be close by."

Christina liked a man who felt that kind of concern for those he cared about. Even a horse. She imagined that translated to people as well. Nelson had felt none of that in regard to her, and they had been together for four years. In fact, he had thrown her to the wolves to protect himself.

Along with Nelson had gone her dream of a

husband and children as well. He'd destroyed all her business and personal dreams.

She didn't want it to get back to Dr. Dillard she hadn't been a team player. Enough that she wouldn't make any ripples by insisting he stay elsewhere. With her work at the Derby, she could make great contacts that would help her rehabilitation program grow. If Gold won the Derby it would also put her farm on the map just because he had stayed there.

And she could use the money. She was trying to build her business. That money could be put to good use. Part of her rehabilitation program was the water program she had developed and invested in. The heated pool for horses had put her back financially but it would pay for itself in a few years. Or at least that was the plan. She hoped one day Seven Miles Farm and Stables would be synonymous with the best place to take horses for rehabilitation and rest.

"Okay, but only twice the amount. Three times makes me feel dishonest."

He huffed.

They exited the barn into the afternoon sunlight.

Conor stopped and looked around the area.

She rested her hands on her hips and squinted against the bright spring afternoon sun. Did he see what she did? The beauty of the long tree-lined drive. The emerald green of the grass. The brilliance of the white wood fences. She loved the area around Versailles, Kentucky. For her, there was no other place in the world.

"It is pretty here. More than I imagined it would be."

Christina heard the sadness in his voice. "But you're already missing home."

"Something like that. This wasn't a trip I wanted to make." She had the distinct feeling his perceptive look missed very few details.

"You don't have to be here long. Only three weeks. It will pass fast. Especially Derby week."

"I'm counting on that." His face remained a mask, showing none of the emotion his tone indicated.

For some reason his attitude made her sad. But it wasn't her job to see about him; it was to board Gold. That was what she should focus on. She shouldn't see much of him. Her job had her keeping early mornings and late evenings. There was also her regular practice to see about. For the trouble there would be great gain. What could go wrong?

Conor watched the expression on Christina's face change from shock to thoughtful to acceptance.

He had Gold stabled, and he was ready to get some rest as well. All the traveling had left him tired and irritable. "If you don't mind, I really am exhausted. If you'd just point me in the direction of where I am to stay, I'll head there."

That shook her out of whatever was running through her mind and started her toward the barn's open doors to the outside.

Conor was quickly running out of good humor. He opened his mouth to say he would stay in the barn, but he thought better of it. "I assure you I am not an axe murderer. You are safe with me. I promise. I'm too tired to attack anyone."

"I wasn't thinking—"

"Look. I have no car. Until I pick up my rental tomorrow. I don't know anyone in the US. I don't know my way around."

She rolled her eyes. "I'm not scared of you. I want you to know I'm putting you in the extra room off the kitchen. It's little more than a storage room."

"That sounds fine. At this point I don't care."

Indecision flickered in her eyes.

What had made this woman so scared of men? "I promise I'm a good guy. I'll stay out of your way."

"Then come on up to the house. I'll show you your room." She walked in the direction of the one-level sprawling brick house.

A black truck with supply boxes built on both sides of the bed had been parked near the back door. Conor followed her up the two brick steps into the house. They entered a pale green kitchen. There were dishes in the sink of the same color. On the wood table that looked well-worn lay a pile of envelopes. On the green countertops were the usual appliances such as a coffeemaker, mixer and toaster.

Somehow, this retro look suited her. Yet, he had the idea it wasn't intentional. More like modernizing the kitchen fell low on her to-do list.

She turned down a small hall off the kitchen and entered a room. "This way is your room, or that might be an exaggeration. It's more like a large closet with a bed."

He joined her.

She was busy stacking boxes against the wall so there was a path to a bed. "Sorry about the mess."

A small bed of sorts sat in a corner. There was also a desk and chair. The only item that leaned toward modern was a flat-screen TV on a stand.

"I'm sorry there's not more to it. I just didn't realize that I was gonna be boarding a horse as well as a man."

For someone who didn't want him staying with her, she apologized a lot. The room was so small he could smell the sweetness of hay and lavender on her. The scents of home. "I appreciate it." Conor dropped his leather bag to the floor.

"Thanks. Beggars cannot be choosers. I'm not going to complain."

"The bed is made but I'll have to get you some clean towels." She brushed by him.

His body tensed. The reaction strange yet familiar. It had been a long time since he felt anything for a woman. Conor didn't want to now. He wouldn't be unfaithful like his father had been. She needed to leave. He forced out, "Thanks, I appreciate it."

Christina grabbed a couple of towels from her bathroom closet and returned to the small room. She slowly approached, listening. "Conor?"

Hearing no sound or movement, she stepped to the door. She found him sprawled on the too-small bed, facedown. A soft snore came from him.

It had been over a year since there had been a man sleeping in the house. Until today, she had intended for it to stay that way forever. Nelson had made her hesitant about trusting anyone. Conor wouldn't be around long enough for it to matter. His money would be worth the chance.

After placing the towels on the desk, she took a blanket from the end of the bed and draped it over him. Apparently, he had had all he could take for the day.

Christina headed out the back door. There were still chores to do. Feeding the horses and securing the barn for the night must happen no matter what.

Who was this Irish stranger with the sad eyes now staying in her home?

The next morning the house was still quiet when Christina went out the back door at daylight to take care of the horses. Her guest had not arisen yet. She quickly scribbled a note stating, *Make yourself at home*. Then she left.

A bitterness that hadn't eased much over the past months filled her. She wouldn't be in this position of having a houseguest if it hadn't been for Nelson. Because of him, she was fighting to regain her good reputation and her aspirations and bank account. As if that hadn't been enough, Nelson had almost been the cause of her losing her veterinarian license.

One piece of paper had saved her, or she would have been working elsewhere. Not doing what she loved. That paper had proven she hadn't been the one stealing the drugs. She had to give Nelson kudos; he had been good at covering his problems. She'd no idea what he had been doing behind her back.

Worse, she'd believed he would be her future. Even the father of her children. Which she desperately wanted.

She had been deeply hurt once, and had no in-tention of letting that happen to her again on a professional or personal level. She kept any relationships on a superficial plane. She wouldn't permit another man to crush her like Nelson had. The fact she had managed to salvage her practice and her business was the only thing that had saved her sanity.

Even worse still, when she was down, all her mother could say was how disappointed she had been in Christina's judgment. Her mother reminded her in detail that Christina didn't dress like a lady or have a job where she could have pretty nails. That she lived in a man's world, and the list went on. That if Christina had tried harder, Nelson wouldn't have had to turn to drugs. All she had wanted from her mother had been her support, and there had been none.

Enough of those thoughts. She needed to get moving, there were chores to finish, then horses to exercise and more horses on her schedule to see. She finished feeding the horses and spoke to Gold on her way out. She would let Conor handle him. He really was a fine-looking horse. She couldn't afford to have anything go wrong with him in her barn.

Breakfast for her came before exercising the horses. Closing the kitchen door behind her, she inhaled the smell of coffee. She toed off her boots and left them lying beside the door. She padded across the kitchen floor with nothing but thoughts of her morning cup of coffee.

She pulled up short. Conor stood in front of the range with a fork in his hand. His hair looked damp. Apparently, he had found the bathroom. A worn jean shirt covered his wide shoulders, and the same type of jeans his muscular legs. His feet were bare. As enticing as he looked, she didn't care for how comfortable he appeared in her personal space.

He glanced over his shoulder. "I took you at your word and made myself at home. I haven't eaten since yesterday morning. I made enough for you as well."

"I'm surprised you found anything to fix a meal with." She moved to see what was in the pan.

"It was pretty slim pickings, but I do like a challenge."

Shame filled her. "I'm not much of a cook but I'll try to get by the grocery store today, tomorrow at the latest."

"If you'll tell me where the store is, I'll take care of that after I pick up my rental. It's the least I can do. Especially since you weren't expecting me."

Who was this man who just showed up and cooked her a meal then agreed to buy groceries? He wasn't like anyone else she knew.

"You have about ten minutes before it's ready. You might like to take a look in the mirror."

Christina's hair was a mess. That sounded too much like her mother. "I've been working in the barn, and this is my house. I'm sorry I don't look like I came out of a fashion magazine."

His hands came up in a defensive measure. "Ho, I didn't mean to insult you. I just thought you might like to know you have dirt on your face."

She stomped to the bathroom and looked in the mirror. A large black smear went across her left cheek. Conor's statement had been a nice way of keeping her from going out on her rounds looking foolish. Most people wouldn't have been as considerate. She owed him an apology.

Conor looked up from where he was placing a mug of coffee on the table. "You look neat and tidy."

"I'm sorry I overreacted. Thanks for telling me. I'd have hated to spend all day with dirt on my face."

"No problem," he said as if he had already forgotten it happened.

She glanced around the room. "Talk about neat. You've made a difference in here in a short amount of time."

"I hope you don't mind. I wasn't always tidy. My wife made me learn."

Of course, he had a wife. A man who looked as good as he did, liked animals and was kind enough to help someone out and cooked wouldn't remain unattached for long. A woman would be quick to snatch him up. "I'm sure she misses you."

Clouds filled his eyes and he looked away. "I'm sure it's more like I miss her. She died three years ago."

"Oh, I'm sorry."

"She was a good woman who died far too early. I miss her every day."

The pain in his voice said it was more like every minute. What would it be like to have someone care that much about her? To feel that love and connection so deeply it would still bring sadness to his eyes after you had died.

Nelson had professed that love but in the end they were just words. Their relationship had turned one-sided. His largest interest had been himself. Once she would have liked to have an unbreakable connection with someone, but the chances of that happening were gone. Now she didn't trust her judgment enough to let a man into her life.

CHAPTER TWO

CONOR COULD NOT believe he had just told an almost perfect stranger about his wife. It was the most he had shared about Louisa in years. Yet, he thought of her daily. Remained devoted to her even after she had done something as selfish as committing suicide. But he could never talk about the loss of their child.

That was something his father never gave his mother. Devotion. When his mother had been alive or dead. Conor had watched his mother slowly drift away, become a shell of herself in her humiliation over his father's public infidelity. As a boy, Conor had vowed to remain true to his wife. He had kept that promise even after her death. That conviction drove his personal life. When he made a commitment, it stood for something.

He had tried to keep his pain and thoughts over Louisa to himself. In an odd way it had felt good to let go of even one detail about her. Maybe that was what his family had been wanting him to do for the past few months. They saw what he needed even if he couldn't. But guilt rose in him. The worst was he had noticed Christina as a woman, causing the guilt to swamp him, but he could not help himself.

Like now, as he watched her move around the kitchen. Her actions fascinating him. He had missed that part of being with someone the most. Having another person around. The peace of knowing someone was nearby. Maybe that was it, the reason he had been comfortable enough to tell Christina about Louisa. He had nothing to worry about. It had nothing to do with attraction and everything to do with his needing someone to talk to.

"I must exercise the horses and then I've got some rounds to make this afternoon."

Christina's statement brought him out of his perplexing thoughts. "Mind if I get a ride to the car rental place? I understand it's not far from here."

"Sure." Having finished her meal, she pushed back from the table. "Leave the dishes. I'll clean up later."

"I'll get them today."

Christina shrugged. "I appreciate it."

"I'll be out to check on Gold in just a few minutes."

She set her dishes in the sink. "Thank you for breakfast."

"You're welcome." She headed out the back door as if she was already thinking about what she had to do for the day.

Conor wasn't sure he liked being dismissed or why it bothered him that she did so.

Fifteen minutes later he had finished tidying the kitchen as much as he could without invading her personal space. He pulled on his boots and walked to the barn.

Outside he took a deep breath, bringing the fresh spring air into his lungs. He scanned the countryside. If he couldn't be in his beloved Ireland, then this part of the world must be the next best place. He continued to the barn. Gold would be glad to see him. He had agreed to fill in as groom as well.

Gold's trainer would arrive by the end of next week in time for Gold to move to the barns on the backside of Churchill Downs. The trainer had other horses he worked, and he could not be away for weeks. Gold's trainer intended for the horse to have a couple of weeks' rest before he started serious workouts. The idea was to have Gold eager to race.

Christina walked one of the other horses back into a stall as he entered the barn. "That's a fine-looking animal."

She patted the horse on the neck and closed

the gate between her and the animal. "Yeah, this is Honey."

The horse did have a coat that reminded Conor of warm honey.

"She's staying with me because of a torn tendon."

"That's pretty difficult to repair." Conor was surprised she was even trying. It was an expensive and long process, if it worked.

"It is, but that's what this farm is all about, or at least it will be."

He walked over to pet Gold's nose hanging over the stall gate. "I thought you just boarded horses."

"No, I'm working to build this into a rehabilitation farm for racehorses. I'm just boarding Gold as a favor for the track vet."

"I understand." He opened Gold's stall and entered.

Christina went to another stall. She walked the horse out of the barn.

Conor fed Gold before leading him outside to the padlock where Christina was circling the horse on a lead rope. As the horse went around the space so did she. Her movements were easy and graceful.

She glanced in his direction.

Had she caught him staring? He continued to the mechanical hot walker. After attaching Gold to one of the arms of the merry-go-round-looking contraption, he started the motor. Gold was led around, getting his exercise. Conor returned inside to muck out Gold's stall.

Christina entered the barn, tied the horse to the gatepost and proceeded to brush the horse.

Conor became caught up in her actions once again. Each stroke was smooth and careful. She made long ones across the horse's back that had him bowing his back. What would it be like to have her do that across his body?

Was he losing his mind? He hadn't had those type of thoughts in years. Why this woman? Why now? Maybe she should be afraid of him.

Conor held himself back from rushing out of the barn. He took his time returning with Gold. Thank goodness by the time he did Christina was nowhere in sight. He groomed Gold in peace, but still glimpses of Christina's attentions flashed in his mind as he worked. Was it wrong to be jealous of a horse?

For lunch Christina put out bread and sandwich meats. She ate at a desk on the other side of the room while on the computer. He sat at the table reading an equine magazine he was not familiar with.

She turned in her chair. "I'm leaving in about twenty minutes if you want a ride to the rental car place."

He closed the magazine. "I'll be waiting by the truck."

* * *

She asked as he climbed out of the truck at the rental place, "Can you find your way back?"

"Yes, I've been paying attention and I have GPS." It was the first concern she had shown him.

She nodded, a slight smile on her lips. "GPS doesn't always work well around here."

"I'll keep that in mind. Thanks for the ride."

Christina wasn't home when he returned. He spent the rest of the day getting settled into his small office slash make-do bedroom. He stacked boxes around and cleaned off a space on the desk for himself. Would Christina mind him doing so? She was so different from Louisa, but for some reason he found Christina interesting. He wasn't sure if he was comfortable with those feelings or not.

The next afternoon Christina pulled up her drive and circled into her regular parking spot behind the house beside Conor's red rental truck. She had been gone all afternoon doing rounds and hadn't seen him all day. He'd already left by the time she had returned to the house after seeing to the horses that morning. Her breakfast waited on the table. A carafe of hot coffee sat there as well. Where he had gone so early in the morning she couldn't imagine, but that wasn't any of her business. Yet, that didn't keep her from wondering.

She climbed out, immediately noticing the barn doors were open. She had closed them securely that morning. Maybe Conor had gone out there and failed to secure them since then.

She walked to the barn, entering with the late-afternoon sun streaming in from the other side.

Wind, one of her boarded horses, stood in the hallway tied to the post of a stall gate. Conor was squatted down on his haunches, looking at the horse's leg. He ran his hand along the leg, pausing at the knee joint.

Her concern turned to anger. What was he doing? This horse had been entrusted to her. He had no business touching him or having the horse out of the stall. Some of her boarders were temperamental and could easily run. What if one of them got away?

She started toward him.

He looked up. "Hello."

"What exactly is going on here?" She heard the bite in her voice. Did he? She stepped closer.

"He has a wound. I brought him out because the light is better."

"You could have just waited to tell me. This horse is in my charge. The owners don't like just anyone touching them."

Conor stood to his full height and squared his shoulders. "If I was the owner, I would appreciate help where I could get it."

"These horses' owners want a veterinarian seeing to their animal. Pardon me but not a trainer or groom."

Conor's eyes bore into hers as if he were speaking to a simpleton. "Many trainers and grooms are better equine caregivers than a veterinarian. That being said, despite your lowly opinion of me, I am a veterinarian."

Her brows went up. He was? She had assumed he was a groom sent over to see about Gold. It had never crossed her mind a veterinarian would have come all the way from Ireland with a horse.

"I am here at the request of the owner. I've taken care of Gold since he was a colt. His owner wanted me to travel with Gold since he can have a temper, and this is a new environment for him, but he knows me. I assure you I'm more than capable of taking care of Gold or any other horse you have in your stable."

"I'm…uh…sorry. I didn't mean to insult you."

"What about grooms and trainers?" His look chastised.

"Or them, either. It's just that I'm responsible for these horses and I can't afford for anything to happen to them on my watch. I guess I'm pretty proprietorial."

"I would say you are." His attention returned to the horse's leg.

That didn't sound like a compliment.

"But that can be a positive or a negative." He softened his earlier words. His deep Irish brogue went a long way toward easing her frayed nerves.

"Back to this horse." He touched the horse lightly. "The wound on his foreleg needs to be debrided and cleaned then wrapped."

"Let me have a look." Christina went to one knee and examined the leg. "This is pretty deep. I think stitches are required."

"I disagree. You are too quick to add something that isn't natural. A good cleaning with antiseptic and a bandage should do well. It isn't that deep. Let nature take its course."

She stood. "I should be the judge of that. I'm the one responsible for the animal, not you."

"Yet, I have some knowledge in these matters."

She placed her hands on her hips. "And you're saying I don't?"

"I'm not saying that at all. I'm just saying you might be overtreating."

His calm words only irritated her. "I don't agree. I would appreciate it if you would step away and leave me to this."

"What can I do to help you?" He coolly watched her.

She huffed. "I'm going to need some heated water. You can go to the house and see to that."

"Sending me off to get me out of the way?"

"Just pretend you're preparing for the delivery

of a baby." Christina didn't miss the darkening of his face before he swiftly turned and stalked out of the barn. What had she said to upset him?

She would have to worry about his attitude later. There was work to do now. She went to the large enclosed room in the barn where she stored all her medical supplies and tack for the horses. After entering, she gathered bottles of saline, bandages, a tube of anti-infection cream and placed them in a cardboard box before going to the locked box that held her injectable medicines.

This was one part of her world she kept in order by the alphabet. And kept a count of. What was an S drug doing in the Ws? She must have knocked it out of place. Those types of occurrences she'd never questioned until Nelson's stunt. Now she found problems everywhere.

Had Conor been in here for some reason? He didn't even have a key. With a shrug, she returned the vial to its correct position and took out a vial of antibiotic. She also grabbed a syringe in a plastic cover. Picking up a bowl, she headed back to Wind.

Wind stomped as she set the box down to retrieve a four-legged stool and placed it nearby. "Easy, boy, this will be over soon."

Christina found the suture kit and opened it, removing the scissors. "I'm going to cut away the skin. Hold still and it'll all be over soon." She snipped pieces of dead skin off.

Conor entered the barn with a pan in his hand, but she didn't slow her work. Wind shifted to the right, but Christina held tight to his foot.

With a quick movement Conor placed the pan on the floor and came around her to hold Wind's head. He whispered to the horse in a low, smooth voice. Conor's gentle brogue rippled over her as well.

She did like his accent. What would it be like to have him whisper in her ear? She shivered just to think of the possibility. Where did that bizarre thought come from? It was not something that would ever happen, but still a girl could dream.

She'd had dreams but they'd been shattered. At one time, she had believed that there would be a forever-after between her and Nelson. They'd made plans to marry, and then she learned of his duplicity. At least this time she had been smart enough to put the house and farm in her name. Nope, she was better on her own. She would keep it that way.

Finished with the skin removal, she brought the pan close and dipped a rag into the warm water and washed the area around the wound, removing a piece of hay, dirt and grit. All the while she worked Conor spoke to the horse, keeping him distracted from what she was doing.

Christina patted the front thigh of the horse then picked up the bottle of saline and opened it. "This next bit might not be too much fun but hang in there, Wind."

Conor changed his stance, taking a more secure hold on the horse's head.

"There we go, boy," she spoke to the horse. Turning the bottle up, she let the fluid flow over the wound, washing any debris away. She continued until it was all gone, then looked carefully for anything in the wound. There couldn't be any chance for infection.

"You want a second set of eyes?"

"Yeah, sure. I could use a leg stretch, too."

"Then change places with me." He offered his hand to help her up.

She hesitated a moment, then placed her hand in his. A shock of electric awareness went through her. She quickly let his hand go. He moved closer to take her seat. Conor smelled of citrus, hay and grain. Like the countryside.

He handed her the lead rope before he stepped away from her. Lifting the horse's foot, he braced it on his knee.

Christina watched the top of Conor's head as he looked at the wound. Her fingers itched to touch his thick hair, but she resisted. Setting the foot on the floor, he took a seat on the stool and picked up the tube of ointment. "Nice job. The trimming and cleaning are excellent work."

Christina couldn't help but glow under his praise.

He glanced at her. "I'll finish if that's okay with you."

"I'm still not convinced that it doesn't need to be stitched."

Conor's look met hers and held. "Trust me."

Trust wasn't something that Christina gave easily, if at all. Nelson had destroyed that ability. "I'm just supposed to trust your word on this?"

"Yes." His tone didn't waver.

She couldn't have him messing around with her horses. "Their owners trusted me. If something goes wrong, I'm the one with her name and business on the line." What she didn't say was she had already had that happen and that one time had been enough. She was having to re-earn her good name.

"I'm telling you that nothing will go wrong. In fact, my way is easier on the horse. You try my way for twenty-four hours and then you can do it your way."

He made it sound like he was the one calling the shots. "If there isn't improvement by the morning, I'll be stitching him up."

Conor said nothing. He pulled on plastic gloves

and smeared antibacterial ointment on his finger and applied it to Wind's leg.

The horse flinched, its skin rippling. Christina held the halter snugger. "Easy, boy, it's almost over."

Conor sat the medicine aside and picked up the paper-covered gauze and began wrapping the leg in a sure neat manner born of practice. He worked with swift efficiency.

"That should do it." He stood and stretched, raising his hands above his head.

Despite her best effort, Christina couldn't help but watch.

He finished and his look met hers.

She had been caught staring. Why he interested her, or why she even cared about him knowing she'd been watching him, she didn't know. Still, a tingle shot through her, and she looked away. "I'll give him a shot and put him in the stall then clean up. Thanks for your help."

"I don't mind putting things away. See to Wind." He patted the horse on the neck. "You are a good patient, boy."

"That you are." She ran her palm down the horse's nose then tied his lead rope to the post. She drew up the liquid from the vial.

"What're you giving him?"

"Trimethoprim sulfa."

Conor nodded. "That antibiotic should work well."

At least they could agree on that. She injected the needle into the horse's hip. "Before you go back into the stall, I need to see if I can find what caused this."

She went to the tack room. After finding a hammer and flashlight she entered the stall, searching for a nail or piece of metal sticking out. In a methodical order she searched for what might have wounded Wind.

"Got it." A small piece of metal that secured the bottom of the feed trough stuck out. "Wind," she spoke to him over the wall of the stall, "how in the world you managed getting your leg near this I'll never know, but it's the only place I see where you could have gotten hurt."

Conor joined her. "Show me."

She pointed to the spot.

Conor shook his head. "Horses never cease to amaze me."

Christina hammered at the metal to flatten it but it didn't lie against the wood as it should.

Conor put out his hand. "May I?"

"Sure. You're welcome to give it a try." She watched the muscles in his back and arms flex and release as he worked. Were they as hard as they appeared? These thoughts had to stop. Conor was her guest, not on her farm to ogle.

"How's that?"

"Uh…yeah, that looks good. I'll get Wind." She stepped into the hall, glad for the soft breeze blowing through it. Tonight it would rain. Taking Wind's halter she said, "Come on, big boy, I'll get you tucked away for the night."

Conor had the surgery items cleaned away, leaving a small bag of trash neatly tied up on the ground beside the stool and the pan on top. It was nice to have such an efficient man around.

"Anything I need to do?" he asked.

"I need to put the antibiotic in the refrigerator." She went to the tack room and placed the vial in the small refrigerator she kept there for just this reason. On her way out she picked up a folding chair and carried it with her.

She unfolded it near the gate to Wind's stall.

Conor stood behind her. "What are you doing?"

"I'm going to sit up for a while to make sure no heat sets in around the wound."

"You can't take the bandage off until the morning. The more you open it the less likely it is to heal well."

She cut her eyes at him. "I know that."

He lowered his head, acting contrite. "Sorry. I'm sure you do. I'll take the pan and trash in."

Twenty minutes later he returned with a basket.

"What're you doing?" She turned in the chair, putting the paperback book she kept in the tack room for these occasions across her knee not to lose her spot.

"I brought us something to eat since we missed dinner and I will not let you sit up alone with our patient." He placed the basket on the floor beside her. "I hope you have another chair put away somewhere."

"In the tack room behind the door."

Conor set up the chair beside her. Picking up the basket, he removed a thermos. "Tea. Hot." He placed that on the floor. "And ham and cheese sandwiches." He handed her one covered in plastic. "Can I pour you some tea?"

"Sure. Thanks for this, Conor. It's very nice of you."

The smile he gave her made her stomach flutter. "You're welcome."

They sat in silence for a few minutes before Conor asked, "Will you tell me what made you decide to become a veterinarian? A large animal veterinarian at that. We don't have many female large animal vets in Ireland."

"We're about fifty-fifty here. As to why, I imagine it was the same things as you. I love animals. I just gravitated to large animals and then horses in particular. Look where I live. It would have been hard not to care for horses."

"I guess it would have."

"Did you grow up on a farm?" Conor watched her face. He liked how expressive her features were.

"Nope. In town with one small dog. Much to my mother's chagrin, I loved horses."

"She doesn't like them?"

Christina rubbed her booted heel in the dirt of the floor. "It was more like she wanted me to be a girly-girl and I was more of a tomboy. Let's just say I didn't always measure up to her expectations. In fact, I still don't."

He took a moment to digest that information. Conor knew well the feeling of disappointment in a parent.

She put her cup down near the leg of the chair. "How about you? Did you grow up on a farm?"

"I did. But I didn't know what I wanted to do until I went to work during the summers, just to have a job, at a local veterinary clinic cleaning out cages. That's when my love of veterinarian work began." It also got him away from the ugliness between his mother and father.

"So what brought you on this trip? I've never known the horse's vet to travel with it and do groom work as well."

"My family encouraged me to come when I was offered this opportunity and Gold's owner insisted. He wanted somebody he could trust with Gold. What I did not expect was not to have a place to stay. I appreciate you giving me a room here. Actually, I have liked doing some physical work. It reminds me of when I worked at the clinic."

She grinned. "You're welcome. Please feel free to muck out as many stalls as you wish."

Conor chuckled. "Thanks for reminding me about what it is to do real veterinarian care."

For the next three hours she checked on Wind at least ten times. More than once, she entered the stall to study the bandaged area for any seepage. Placing her hand on the leg to see if there was heat in the skin caused by infection. He had volunteered a couple of times to do the exam, but she had refused.

They turned quiet and Conor watched as Christina's eyes slowly lowered after she leaned her head back against the chair. She would have a crick in her neck if she remained like that all night.

He studied her. She really was a pretty woman. Not in the goddess-or-movie-star-beauty way, but in the simple, fresh and natural sense. What really made her appealing was her caring heart for animals, her quirky, haphazard way of keeping house and her drive to go after what she wanted. What confounded him the most was that he even noticed those characteristics.

It had been forever since he had sat with someone in a simple setting and been satisfied. Even thoughts of Louisa were not hurtling through his mind. For once, he had to bring her up instead of her always being there. The idea made him both uncomfortable and relieved. He wanted to hang on to Louisa while at the same time it was past time to let her go. Was that how his father had felt about his mother?

He gave Christina's shoulder a shake. "You better go inside or you're going to fall out of the chair."

She mumbled, "I need to stay here and keep an eye on Wind."

"I understand that, but I think we can go inside now. Get a few hours of sleep. He will be all right until morning."

"I better not…"

"If it will make you feel any better, I'll check on him in a couple of hours. You need to get some sleep." He helped her stand. She swayed on her feet, and he placed an arm around her shoulders, pulling her against him. "You are dead on your feet."

"It's my job."

He started her toward the door. "That may be so but I can help. Now, stop arguing and let me get you inside to bed."

"To bed…"

The way she let the words trail off made him

think of a fire, a soft bed and a warm woman against him. He swallowed hard. The guilt. He did not want that. Could not want Christina. More importantly, he wouldn't allow himself the chance of the pain that caring again might bring.

Christina took a moment to look at Wind. "You promise?"

"You have my word. Now, come on, sleepyhead." Conor guided her, arm around her shoulders, to the house, inside and down the hall to her bedroom. He'd never been in there. At the door, he flipped on the light.

She squeaked. "Turn it off. That hurts my eyes."

He did as she said. "Good night, Christina. Get some rest."

Christina murmured something and moved into the room.

Conor grinned as he walked to his little office bedroom. He shook his head. At the brief glimpse of her room, he saw clothes strewn everywhere. A pile of veterinary magazines beside the bed. It hadn't been made, and the covers looked pushed over to one side, as if she had been in a rush when she woke. The woman might be a great veterinarian, but she needed a housekeeper like no one else he knew.

Taking just his boots off then setting his alarm for two hours, he lay on his bed. He had a horse to check on. A promise to keep. The first in many years.

A buzzing sound went off sooner than he wished. He pulled on his boots and headed out the kitchen door to the barn. Fifteen minutes later he was on his way back to the house. Two hours later, after the sun had brought light to the day, Conor entered the barn again.

Christina was there in Wild's stall on her knees. Conor went to his haunches beside her. "What do you think?"

"I think it's better."

His voice took on a teasing tone. "Then I will not tell you I told you so."

She glanced at him, a gentle smile on her lips. "Thank you for that. I would've hated to hear it. We don't go in for the old methods much around here. Little patience or time. Thanks for reminding me that sometimes time helps more than anything."

Had that been true for him? Or had the passage of time just closed him further off from life? He stood. "You are welcome."

She picked up a roll of gauze and began wrapping the leg once more. "This reminder will come in handy when I plan rehabilitation for horses in my program."

He stepped to Wind's head and stroked his

nose. "What type of horse issues are you planning to concentrate on?"

"Any that are leg related. I hate to see a horse put down when there's a chance that they can be saved. Maybe they won't race again but they still have value." She stood and patted Wind on the neck. "Just like this guy. He's worth the time and energy."

Conor patted the horse's neck as her hand passed. She stopped her movement, and he did, too. She quickly pulled hers away.

"I hate to see the waste of such a majestic animal." She picked up a feed bucket and moved to the trough.

"You know you can't save them all." He continued to stroke Wind while he watched her.

"Maybe not but I can try." She poured the feed into the trough.

By the tone of her voice, she believed deeply in helping the horses. Yet, the reality he well knew. "An admirable goal."

Done with the feed she picked up the trash.

Conor smiled and shook his head. Christina might not be a housekeeper, but he could find no fault in her care of the horses, her supply room, or the barn's cleanliness. "Come on. I'll fix us a hot breakfast."

They stepped out of the stall.

"Did you cook when you were married?" Christina asked.

"No. I had to learn after she was gone. Now I enjoy it."

"You know you don't have to cook for me all the time." She went to the gate and pushed it closed, locking it.

He started down the hall beside her. "I know but you're letting me stay here when you had not planned to have company, and I've got to feed myself so I might as well feed you, too."

"I have to admit your cooking is better than cold cereal but I'm gaining weight." She chuckled.

"From what I have seen you'll be just fine with a few extra pounds." He glanced at Christina, who met his look.

"Thanks. That's nice of you to say."

CHAPTER THREE

CHRISTINA WOKE TO the sun shining through the window of her bedroom. She jerked to a sitting position. She never slept this late. The horses would be starving. After being up late two nights ago, her lack of sleep must have caught up with her. The horses were no doubt stomping in their stalls to have their morning feed.

She flipped the covers off and popped out of bed. She didn't bother to remove the T-shirt she wore. Jerking yesterday's jeans on, she zippered and buttoned them and headed for the door. She would dress for the day later. The horses came first.

Not slowing down, she ran into a solid wall of warm, damp flesh. Strong fingers wrapped her upper arms, preventing her from falling backward.

"Umph."

She grabbed Conor's waist to steady herself. That only made the quiver running through her worse.

"Where are you headed in such a rush?" His sexy Irish brogue had deepened despite the spark of humor in it. The warmth of his breath whispered by her ear.

"Morning chores. Running late," she managed to get out.

"All taken care of. I saw to them all this morning when I checked on Wind and Gold."

"How is he?"

"Doing much better. I removed the bandage and checked him and reapplied it. He seems to be comfortable."

Unlike her. Christina stepped back, putting space between them. She now had a clear view of Conor's well-formed bare chest. He must have just finished his shower. She had been better off standing closer to him. She swallowed hard.

"I appreciate the help, but I'll just go out and check on him." She was used to doing everything by herself. She hadn't had help in a long time. Even then it hadn't turned out she could trust it.

"They've all been well cared for but I'm sure you'll want to see for yourself."

At least he didn't sound offended. More like impressed.

He shifted to the side, giving her clear passage. His look dropped lower. He cleared his throat. "I'll see to breakfast."

It wasn't until she pulled on her jacket, she realized he could see through her thin shirt. Even now her nipples remained at attention from being so close to him. Great. She couldn't do anything about it now. With a tug, she put on her boots. In the future she would be more careful.

In the barn she found everything just as it should be. Each animal looked well cared for.

She returned to the house to find Conor sitting at the kitchen table with a cup of coffee in front of him. At the chair to his right waited her coffee. There was also a bowl of oatmeal with toppings sitting on the table. He spoiled her. This attention she would miss when he left.

"I should get a shower before I eat." She stepped toward the door.

"Then your oatmeal will be cold." He sounded disappointed.

"Ugh, I'm not exactly adequately dressed."

His gaze lingered at her chest then came back to meet hers. Her nipples tightened. "I'd say you look just right."

"I still believe I'll change. I'll warm my coffee and oatmeal up."

He wore that slight grin she found so sexy. "If that's the way you want it."

She shivered. Should she be concerned about whatever was not being said between them? Yet, he had never once been anything but a gentleman. In fact, he looked irritated, she noticed. Maybe she was wrong. Her judgment could be off. Nelson had proven that. Still, Conor had been good to her and the horses.

Christina hurried down the hall to the bathroom for a quick hot shower and returned to the kitchen a short while later.

Conor still sat at the table, nursing his cup of coffee, with an *Equine* magazine she had received in the mail the day before open in front of him.

While she warmed her meal he asked, "What are your plans for today?"

"I've some patients to see." She pulled the food out at the beep.

"Mind if I tag along and see how it's done over here?"

Could she spend the entire day with him? She didn't say anything as she sat down to eat.

"This babysitting job is not quite as intensive as it could be. Gold is doing fine."

How could she say no? "I imagine it will be rather dull for you. It's simple basic veterinarian work. But you're welcome to come along if you want."

"I bet I will learn something. I'll straighten up here and be ready to go when you are."

"I've got to load supplies into my truck. I'll be about twenty minutes or so." She started toward the door.

"I need to collect my wallet and jacket." Conor went to his room.

Christina finished her breakfast and hurried out to the barn to get her supplies together. She was inside the tack room looking at the medicine box when Conor walked up.

"Is something wrong?" He came to stand beside her.

"No. I'm just doing my daily count."

"Daily?"

"Yes. I like to keep a close eye on my regulated medicines." Especially after what Nelson did. She couldn't take a chance on anyone ever stealing from her again.

"I also check the truck daily." She closed and locked the metal box attached to the wall.

He stepped into the hallway. "Why such vigilance?"

Christina joined him. "Because I can't afford any controversy. I've been working too hard to get my reputation back."

His brows came together and created a furrow. "What do you mean by that?"

"I'll tell you in the truck. I need to get going if I don't want to work late into the night."

They walked out of the barn.

"Stealing drugs is a real problem. Offenders are good at it." Nelson had been getting away with it for almost a year before she realized what he was doing.

"In Ireland it's the same. We watch ours closely as well. Those days of it just sitting on the shelf unattended are long gone."

She put the few items she needed away in one of the supply compartments on the truck.

He stood at the front of the vehicle. "Anything I can do to help?"

"No. I got it." She stored the medicines and IV needles in a locked bin. "Let me check the horses once more and I'll be ready to go."

"I now understand why Gold was boarded here. You are careful."

Her look met his. "I take what I care about seriously. Don't you?"

Conor did. To the detriment of his heart. Three years later he still honored his marriage vows. Something his father hadn't done. Conor believed in keeping his promises. Would Louisa have wanted or expected that of him for this long? Hadn't it been her choice to leave him? If he stepped out and had interest in a woman, would that be bad? He was tired of being lonely. He had not realized how much so until he'd started staying with Christina. But wouldn't that make him no better than his father? That, Conor wouldn't accept.

Conor climbed into the passenger side of her large truck. What had possessed him to request to go with Christina today? He wasn't sure if it had been out of boredom or being truly interested in the type of veterinary practice she had, or worse, the fact he just wanted to spend more time with her. That last thought gave him a prickly, panicky feeling.

Christina settled in behind the steering wheel. "I have a rather long day today. You're sure you want to go?"

Was she trying to encourage him not to go? "I am. How far do we drive to the first patient?" He buckled up.

"What I like to do is start at my farthest appointment and work my way home unless there is a serious case that needs to be seen right away. About sixty miles is my radius."

"That's half the distance across Ireland in some places. That can make for a long day."

She glanced at him. "Would you like to change your mind?"

"Are you trying to get rid of me?" He made a show of getting comfortable.

Christina started the truck. "Not at all."

She still hadn't relaxed enough for him to question her about the medicines more. He watched the countryside, glancing at her occasionally. She drove with determination.

Before midafternoon, they had stopped at three different farms all with long driveways and miles of wooden fence. At each, the owner or trainer was there to greet Christina when she stopped the truck outside the barn. She grabbed her bag and hopped out, ready to go to work each time.

With a wave of her hand in his direction she would say, "This is Conor O'Brian. He is visiting from Ireland." Her attention would then return to the problem with the horse.

Her efficiency amazed and impressed him as she went about the care of the horse, all the while talking and touching the animal as if they had been friends forever. Why did she insist on hiding all that tenderness behind gruff toughness?

They finished with one farm and were driving to the next. Christina hadn't said more than what was necessary the entire day. Being a veterinarian could be a solitary job but this was ridiculous. "Are you mad at me? Did I do something wrong?"

"Why would you think that?" She tilted her head in question.

He turned in the seat to see her better. "You haven't said over ten words to me in the last three hours."

"I've been thinking."

About what? "Maybe if you talk it out it would be better."

"I don't think that'll work." She slowed and

made a left turn down a tree-lined country road
with fenced green pasture.

"Try it. You never know." He looked at her profile. At least her jaw didn't appear as tight. Either
way, Christina appealed to him. What would she
look like in something feminine? He had certainly
been aware of her breasts in the thin T-shirt that
morning. More so than he'd been in years. Why
Christina and why now?

"I almost lost my license a few years back."

He shifted in the seat, sitting straighter, his attention completely on her.

She glanced at him. "You aren't going to say
anything?"

"No, I figured you'd say more when you were
ready."

A small smile came to her lips. "I was stupid.
Too trusting, really. I should have been doing the
inventory of the medicines since it was my name
on the line. But my then live-in boyfriend of four
years, who I believed I would marry, had been
stealing drugs. He was a vet tech and planning
to enter veterinarian school. Then the authorities caught him selling and everything blew up.
I barely retained my license. I'm still trying to
build my good name back."

"So that's why you count the medicine daily.
You blame yourself for his mistakes."

"That's pretty close to it."

He could hear the shame in her voice. "I'm sorry to hear that. It must have been hard to have believed in someone and have them let you down." How many times had he watched his father do that to his mother?

"It was."

Christina pulled into a small roadside park. Horses stood in the field surrounding them, swishing their tails in the bright sunlight. She faced him.

"I had just gotten the idea for opening a rehabilitation farm for racehorses and had started to look for funding. All the banks had gotten the word about what happened, so that was a no-go. Nelson, that was my ex, had not only destroyed my regular world but had managed to do the same to my dreams. That's why I agreed to take Gold so I could get in good with Dr. Dillard at Churchill Downs. I want to be one of the veterinarians on duty during the Derby. That's a prestigious position. It will look good on my vitae. I can also make contacts with those who might use my farm for not only rehabilitation but for horse holidays." She pulled two protein bars out of the pocket of the driver's door, handing one to him. "Break time."

His brows rose. He took it and unwrapped it. "Horse holidays?"

Her first smile of the day. "You know, a place to stay during downtime."

"That's sort of what this trip has been for me."

"How's that?"

Conor took a bite out of his bar and chewed slowly, trying to stall having to answer. Why had he said that about coming to America? After Christina had shared her own story, he owed her at least part of his. But he couldn't give her all. That, he wouldn't talk about. The loss of his baby was too painful.

"You have heard most of it. About my family wanting me to be here. Because they don't think I'm moving on after my wife's death."

"Are you?"

He'd never really thought about it. How like Christina to cut to the center of the problem. He would like to say he had started moving on but he couldn't. "I don't know."

She studied him a moment. "I bet you do."

"They thought I kept to myself too much. They wanted me to visit old friends, go to the pub, or come to their house for parties."

"But you didn't, did you?"

He shook his head. "Mostly I saw my patients and stayed at home. Then it became one patient. Gold. That might have ended if William Guinness had not insisted he wanted me taking care of Gold." Even to Conor that sounded sad. "I've been around more people since I came here than I have been in a year."

"I guess them pushing you to come worked."

He gave her a wry smile. "I guess it did."

Christina's phone rang and she clicked the hands-free speaker in the truck. "Doctor Mobbs."

"This is Dr. Dillard at Churchill Downs. I was wondering if you could come by and see me sometime today at the clinic."

Christina's eyes widened. Maybe this was what she'd been waiting on. "Sure, I can be there in about thirty minutes."

"I will expect you then."

She hung up. To Conor she said, "I hope you don't mind a trip to the racetrack. I need to obviously have a conversation with Dr. Dillard."

"I don't mind at all. Do you know what it's about?" His eyes held concern.

"I hope it's about me being on staff during Derby week." Christina pushed down her excitement.

"Why does that matter so much to you?"

"For one thing it's an honor. It also says that I'm a good enough veterinarian to be a part of that group." She started the truck.

"And you doubt you are good enough?"

"No, but others might." She wanted to move off that subject. She wasn't ready to go into why working at the Downs was so important to her.

Instead, she shared the reason she could utter. She wasn't ready to go into how she had disappointed her mother. How her mother had thought Christina had dragged their name in the mud with the business with Nelson when it made the news. "It's a golden opportunity for me to tell other veterinarians about my new program. They will hopefully refer our horses to my farm."

"I get that."

"The Derby is the greatest event in Kentucky each year. It's like the English have Ascot. Hundreds of thousands will be there in person, and millions will watch it on TV."

"I had no idea it was so big. The racetrack is massive."

She glanced at him. "You've been to Churchill Downs?"

"Yes. I had to go see about a stable for Gold. Check out where he would be staying. I made arrangements to have him examined and tested before he could be boarded there. I also checked in with the vet clinic to make sure I knew exactly what was expected testing-wise."

Before now she hadn't thought much about what Conor had been doing with his days. "You've been a busy guy. And here I thought you spent your days planning my meals."

He grinned. "That doesn't take me hours."

She smiled. "I'm glad because then I'd feel obligated to feel guilty."

They took the wide highway out of the rural area into the large busy city of Louisville. She entered the Churchill Downs grounds and drove around to the backside.

"You've been here before?"

"Numerous times." She pulled into a parking spot near a large building.

"Do you mind if I come in with you?"

"No, that's fine." Christina didn't wait on him before she headed toward the door of the Churchill Downs Equine Medical Center.

"I want to check out the facilities up close." He caught up with her and followed her into the building.

"Then I'll see you in a few minutes," she said over her shoulder before she spoke to the woman behind a desk just inside the door. "I'm Christina Mobbs. I'm here to see Dr. Dillard."

"Give me just a minute. He's seeing a horse right now." The woman walked down a hall toward the back of the building.

Christina took a seat in one of the two plastic chairs against the wall in the small reception area. Conor sat beside her.

She clasped and unclasped her hands. She couldn't help being nervous.

He said softly, "Hey, you have no reason to be so nervous. You'll wear the skin off your hands."

She narrowed her eyes.

"From what I've observed of your work you're as good as anyone I've ever seen. You're excellent with the horses, and your veterinarian work is superb. Don't ever let anybody make you feel any differently. It'll be fine." He placed his hand over her wringing hands for a moment.

That tingle she had when he touched her shot through her again. She gave him an unsure smile. "Thanks for that vote of confidence. It's been a long time since someone encouraged me."

A barrel-chested doctor walked toward them. Christina quickly stood. "Doctor Dillard, it's good to see you again."

"You, too," Dr. Dillard said. He glanced at Conor.

She turned to Conor. "I understand you've met Doctor O'Brian."

"Yes. Good to see you again." The two men shook hands. "Doctor O'Brian, please feel free to observe wherever you like while I speak with Doctor Mobbs. Doctor Mobbs, if you would come with me. We'll meet in my office."

Conor gave Christina a reassuring smile before she walked away with Dr. Dillard.

Christina appreciated Conor's encouragement. She'd had little of that in her life and even less in the past few years. Now that she could look back at it realistically, Nelson hadn't provided that, either. She had been the one who kept the farm and their relationship moving. Nelson rarely offered her help or encouragement. She'd wanted marriage and children. He dragged his feet. Why she'd waited until he almost destroyed her entire world to distance herself from him, she would never know.

She certainly hadn't looked to her mother for praise. Her father said little to contradict her mother. To Christina's surprise, Conor's kind words were the most she could remember hearing in a long time. It took a stranger from halfway around the world for her to start believing in herself again.

"This is more a closet than an office but it's the best they could give me out here," Dr. Dillard said as he led her through a doorway.

"It's not a problem." Christina entered the room.

"Doctor O'Brian seems like a good fella. Thank you for being willing to board the horse he's overseeing."

"My pleasure." Conor really had been a good houseguest. She couldn't stop herself from enjoying having another person around. And he wasn't hard to look at, either. It was nice to have someone in her corner, too. A surge of pleasure went through her at the memory of his supportive smile. "Gold is acclimating well. Doctor O'Brian has been good help as well."

"When I spoke to him the other day, he said he was pleased with staying at your farm. I'm glad to hear that." Dr. Dillard cleared his throat. "Why I asked you here is to speak to you about joining the vet team during Derby week."

Christina's heart beat faster. "I would appreciate the opportunity."

He nodded. "You'll be doing different assignments leading up to the race days and on those you'll be stationed along the racetrack."

"I look forward to helping out." At least she would get a chance to watch the races. Some veterinarians would remain in the barn area, unable to see anything.

Dr. Dillard's eyes turned concerned. "Will you be able to handle your practice and farm while being here for a week?"

"I'll make that work."

"You'll need to be here before daylight and you'll be staying until after dark." Dr. Dillard wore an earnest look.

She straightened. "That won't be a problem."

"There'll be over forty veterinarians here on Friday and Saturday. We'll have a big responsibility here."

"I'll be glad to be one of them." She meant it.

"And we'll be glad to have you. By the way, next weekend on Saturday night my wife and I are hosting a cookout at our place for the team of veterinarians working at the Downs during Derby week. You should get an invitation in the mail this week. Why don't you bring along Doctor O'Brian as well?"

Christina wasn't sure she wanted to show up as a couple at Dr. Dillard's party but she really didn't have a choice. "I'll be sure to ask him."

"And I'll see you for the party and then on the Monday morning afterward for an orientation meeting here at the Downs." Dr. Dillard smiled at her.

She returned it. "I'll be here."

Christina left the office with a light step. She could hardly wait to tell Conor. She reached the front to find him talking to the woman behind the desk. He left the woman with a smile and joined Christina. She continued out the door and stopped out of sight of those in the clinic.

"Well, are you going to be working the Derby?" he asked, facing her, anticipation in his eyes.

"Yes." She threw her arms around his neck. "I am."

Conor's arms came around her, holding her tight against his hard chest. She absorbed his heat and strength for a moment before she realized what she had done. Letting go, she placed her hands on his shoulders and stepped back. He let his hands fall to his sides.

Her face heated and she looked at the tips of her boots. "I'm sorry. I didn't mean to do that. I was just so excited to tell someone."

"Don't be. That's the nicest thing that has happened to me in a long time."

She glanced up. Conor watched her with a warm intensity that made her belly flutter. "Doctor Dillard wants me to bring you along to a party at his house next Saturday."

He hesitated and looked away before he put more space between them. "Let me think about it."

She hadn't realized until then how much she had liked the idea of their going to a party together, despite her own reservations. Did he just not like parties or was it that he didn't want to go with her? Either way his answer shouldn't have bothered her as much as it did.

"Are we headed home now or out to more stops?" Conor looked everywhere but at her.

"I'm going to stop in and see if my cousin is here. She sometimes helps out at the human clinic." Christina turned toward a small white building down the dirt and gravel road that led farther into the backside. "It's been a while since I've seen her."

He fell into step beside her. "This is really some

place. The spires are impressive. You told me it was large, but I had no idea."

He acted as if nothing had happened a few minutes earlier. If Conor could do that so could she. "I love this place. My cousin's parents used to bring me here occasionally. Not on Derby Day but on weekends just to watch the horses run. I am still amazed by the beauty and majesty of the Thoroughbreds' movements."

"You make it sound like poetry."

She looked at him. "Isn't it?"

"I've never thought about it, but now I have I couldn't agree with you more. One thing we do share is the love of a good horse. There's nothing like watching a morning stretch."

"We call it the Breeze. That's one of the many reasons I can't just let old racehorses go. I want them to have another life after racing. We all deserve a second chance."

His eyes met hers. Admiration filled them. "I think it's a very admirable thing you're doing."

She stopped. "Thank you for that. I needed to hear it."

"You're welcome. You should be praised more often. You are a great vet. You really care about your patients." He grinned. "The only thing I can find you fail at is cooking. And housekeeping of course."

That didn't even begin to hurt her feelings. She laughed. "Yes, I fail at both. Much to my mother's chagrin. She would like me to be a homemaker and mother like her. I don't care much for the homemaking, but I would like to be a mother."

His eyes shadowed over and he looked away for a moment before he asked, "Your parents live close by?"

"No, actually in Florida. They retired and moved down there. But my mother stays in touch with her friends here and seems to know all the gossip before I do." She stopped in front of the medical clinic, a building with the door in the middle and two windows to each side. She opened the door. "Callie works here."

He followed her inside.

"Hi, is Callie around?" Christina asked the man behind the desk. At the sound of a squeal Christina looked down the hall. Callie hurried in Christina's direction with her arms open wide.

"To what do I owe this nice surprise?" She wrapped Christina in a hug.

They separated.

"I've been over to see Doctor Dillard."

"And?" Callie looked at Christina with an anxious expectation.

Christina straightened her shoulders and smiled. "I'll be seeing you around on Derby weekend."

"Well, good for you. I'm not really surprised. I think you're more concerned about what happened than others are."

Christina huffed. "Tell that to the licensing

commission. They seemed pretty uptight about it last year."

Callie waved a hand as if she could brush it all away. "That was then and this is now." She looked past Christina to Conor leaning casually against the wall. "Can I help you?"

"He's with me. Callie, this is Conor O'Brian. He's visiting from Ireland. He's staying at the farm seeing about one of the racehorses."

Callie's brows rose as she studied Conor a moment. "Hello."

"Hi." Conor stepped forward but stopped behind Christina.

"Staying at the farm." She had made it a statement instead of a question. Callie studied Conor keenly for a moment.

"Just while Gold acclimates to the weather and settles from the trip over." Why did Christina feel she had to justify Conor's presence? Because it had been over a year since she had anything to do with a man. It was time to get Callie's mind on something else. "How're you doing?"

"Well. Just getting prepared for the onslaught of people for the Derby. As much as I love the races it's super busy around here."

"This isn't even your place to oversee anymore," Christina said.

"I know but I help out when I'm needed. You're

lucky to catch me here today. Langston is running a test today or I wouldn't be here."

"Langston is her husband, who works with preventing brain injuries," Christina explained to Conor.

Callie said, "I can't believe we live so close and don't see each other more."

"We'll have to do something about that. I hear you and Langston are really doing some innovative things with horse-and-rider safety." Christina liked Callie's Texas husband and appreciated his life-changing work.

"I like to think so. Only problem is we seem to work all the time, but we love it."

"Y'all are supposed to be on your honeymoon." Christina couldn't prevent the wistfulness from entering her voice. At one time she believed she'd be married by now. Maybe even have a child.

A silly grin formed on Callie's lips. "Sure, we are."

What would it be like to have someone act like that just at the thought of her? She looked at Conor, who stood with such patience, waiting on her. That wasn't a direction she should consider.

Callie spoke to Conor. "I hope you're enjoying your stay in America."

"I am."

"I'm sure it's quite different from Ireland," Callie said.

"That it is, but it has its appeals just the same."
He glanced at Christina.

Callie's eyes brightened and she studied Christina a moment. "It does now."

Her face heated. Callie had fallen in love with her husband a year ago and she thought everyone should be in love.

A man holding his hand in the palm of his other one hurried into the clinic.

"I got to go." Callie stepped to the man and led him down the hall. "Be sure to pop in and say hi during the Derby."

"Will do." Christina pushed out the door.

Conor walked beside her on the way to her truck. "Did you and Callie grow up together?"

"We saw a lot of each other. Back then she was determined she was going to be a vet but changed her mind and now she does medical research with her husband on sports-related head injuries."

"That sounds like something beneficial to the industry. I do know there are too many head injuries."

They walked toward her truck. "They're doing some really great innovative work. I'm proud of them."

He reached for the passenger door. "I'm sure they are proud of the work you do or plan to do. Your plan for horses is to be admired as well."

How did this man manage in a few words to lessen the self-loathing she had felt for so long?

CHAPTER FOUR

CONOR APPROACHED THE BARN. He'd thought more than once over the past two days about what Christina had said about everyone deserving a second chance. Wasn't that what he needed, too? His siblings had accused him of not moving on. For so long he hadn't felt he could or even wanted to, but since coming to stay at Christina's a week ago, that had slowly been changing.

Conor wished he had a better idea of what caused Christina distress. He might be able to help. But why did it matter? This was someone he hardly knew, and he would be leaving in a couple of weeks. He had no investment here.

He entered the barn and walked through to the other side and out the doors into the sunlight. He found Christina bathing a horse. He stepped up beside her. "I figured I'd find you here."

She jumped and turned. The water hose she held soaked him from middle to his knees.

Horror flashed over her face. She dropped the

hose and pulled the earbud from her ear. "I'm so sorry. You scared me. I didn't hear you."

He gave her a thin-lipped smile.

Then she doubled over in giggles.

The sound filled him with something best called happiness. He loved the tinkling sound. "Did you do that on purpose?"

Christina took control of her laughing and straightened. She looked at him and busted into giggles again.

Conor reached for the hose, but her booted foot came down on it before he could pick it up. She held it to the ground. He pursed his lips and glared. With a swift movement, he lunged. He would show her. Christina's eyes went wide seconds before he wrapped his arms around hers and secured her against his wet front. He held her there letting his damp clothes seep into hers.

"Stop. You're getting me wet." She wiggled, trying to get away.

His manhood reacted to her struggle. Something he'd experienced little of in the past few years until he had met Christina. It both thrilled and worried him. Yet, he didn't release his hold. He teased, "Who got who wet first and then laughed at them?"

She continued to squirm. "I didn't mean to."

"But you meant to laugh at me," he goaded.

She went still. Her gaze met his. He held it,

watching her eyes shift from determination to awareness to questioning. Did she realize how aroused he was?

The need to kiss her had grown with having her so close, touching him; the days of being near her had compounded themselves into a need to taste her.

She blinked. "I did do that." The giggles bubbled again. "I'm sorry. You should have seen your face."

"I was too busy feeling my clothes being soaked." He tugged her closer.

Mischief filled her eyes. She said with complete innocence, "I didn't mean to."

His look held hers. He made himself not focus on her lips. "Maybe not but I'm still wet."

And desiring her. The feeling had been building for days. He'd pushed it down, shoved it away, but there it had been every time he was around Christina. Maybe if he got the unknown out of the way it wouldn't return.

Would she let him kiss her? What if she refused him? She had her own ghosts holding her back. Did he dare take the chance she would reject him? How would he know if he didn't try? He might regret it for the rest of his life if he didn't. There was enough of those in his life already.

His head lowered. His lips touched hers. He released her arms, his hands moving to rest lightly on her hips. Making her captive was not what he wanted. He needed her to want his kiss. Her hands ran up his chest to settle on his shoulders. An electric thrill shot through him at her touch. Christina wasn't pushing him away. She wanted it, too.

He deepened the kiss. Christina returned it. He pressed her closer.

Conor understood then how he had been fooling himself about not needing a woman. How quickly Christina had made his excuses lies. Every nerve ending in his body hummed with awareness of her. She made him feel alive once more.

She sighed and wrapped her arms around his neck, pressing herself into his throbbing length. Conor slowly kissed the seam of her lips. His tongue traced it, requesting entrance. Pleasure washed through him when she opened her mouth. He savored the warm moment, then plunged forward, eager for more. She welcomed him. His hands caressed her hips and circled to cup her behind, lifting her to him.

He would take all she would offer him. His body hummed like it hadn't in too long, in ways he had forgotten existed. Christina had managed to make him push past his pain.

The whinny of the horse nearby broke them apart.

Christina looked as shocked as he felt. He had to straighten this out. Say something. Reassure her he wouldn't take advantage of her. "I'm sorry. That was inappropriate. I shouldn't have done that. Excuse me."

Disbelief turned disappointment filled her eyes. A flicker of hurt flashed in them before he turned and walked off, guilt washing over him.

Christina watched Conor stalk away, stunned. What had just happened? With him. With her. This wasn't something she'd seen coming. Or had she? Wasn't she attracted to him? She would be lying if she said she hadn't noticed his wide shoulders, his beautiful eyes, or how supportive of her he had been. And that list didn't include his accent that sent shivers down her spine any time he spoke. That had her thinking things she shouldn't. Before going to bed and in her dreams.

Still, she had never expected him to kiss her. Apparently, he hadn't anticipated it, either. Conor acted disgusted that he had kissed her, that he had made the first move. She didn't appreciate that at all.

Having been used before by Nelson and not measuring up to her mother's expectations enough in her life, Christina had no intentions of feeling that way again. Then along came Conor and she had opened herself up once more to rejection. He had slipped through a crack of crazy loneliness, and she'd welcomed him, basking in the feeling of being admired.

She picked up the hose and ran the water over the horse's back. Picking up the sponge, she soaped the horse down.

Maybe their interaction had been a bad idea but the kiss had been amazing. Perfect, in fact. His lips had brushed hers gently then he had crushed her to him as if he might never let her go. In a brief amount of time he had made her feel wanted, desired—necessary. It was as if he sensed what she needed and had agreed to gift it to her.

Then he had abruptly left her. Lost and alone. And not sure all she had felt had been true.

She took in a deep breath of air and let it out slowly. Conor hadn't been completely unaffected. His arousal had been evident between them. That gave her some sense of satisfaction.

A few minutes later she heard the sound of his truck being cranked then the tires over the gravel of the drive. He had left.

He did not return by that evening. She saw to Gold when she made her nightly round.

She had the light off in her room, but she wasn't asleep when Conor returned.

Conor came in quietly, went to his room. He must have taken his boots off because she heard his padded feet in the hall outside her door. His footsteps stopped there.

She held her breath. Would he knock on her door? Was he hoping she was still awake?

Long, lingering moments later, the shower in the bath came on.

Christina rolled her face into the pillow and moaned.

The next morning before breakfast Conor went looking for Christina. It was no surprise he found her in the barn. As he approached, she continued to brush the horse's leg.

From the tension in her shoulders, she was aware he stood nearby. He swallowed hard being fully mindful that she deserved an apology for his actions, during and after their kiss. He shouldn't have done it to begin with and he shouldn't have treated her like she was a mistake.

"Christina?"

"Yes?"

"Can we talk? Clear the air." He stepped closer.

"There's nothing to talk about." She didn't even bother to look at him.

"You know there is."

She faced him. "I've been kissed before. No big deal."

Conor wanted to take her by the shoulders and shake her. Of course, it was more than a kiss. He could still feel the sweetness of her lips beneath his. Had dreamed of doing so again. He cleared his throat. "I shouldn't have walked off like that. I didn't mean to hurt you."

"Don't worry about it. I get it." She didn't look at him.

Conor didn't see how she couldn't worry about it. He had hurt her. "I said some things I shouldn't have. It's just that I promised to be true to my wife."

Her chin dropped and her eyes narrowed as she looked at him as if he had two heads. "I thought she had died."

"She has but I promised to be true."

A compassionate look came to her eyes. Her voice sank low. "Conor, she would want you to go on living. A kiss doesn't mean you're desecrating her memory. It doesn't mean you loved her any less."

He had made a promise he would always be true to Louisa. Not be like his father. But hadn't he used that to build a wall to protect his heart? If he let it down, he might get hurt again. He wasn't sure he could live through that again. Even for Christina.

Christina untied the horse from the post and led it out of the barn.

He watched as she released the animal into the pasture. She slapped the animal on the hip. "Go and have a good day."

The horse ran into the field with his tail in the

air. Wouldn't it be nice if he could do that? Feel free for just a little while?

Conor came to stand beside her. "You care for them like they're your own."

"While they're here, they're my own." She looked at him as if that included him as well.

A lump formed in his chest. "Thank you for caring for Gold last night."

"Not a problem." She made it sound as if it wasn't. Is that the way she saw him, too?

"I know what I do with Gold is important but I'm thankful to you for reminding me of what it is to be a vet again. I've been babysitting one racehorse for so long I've started to forget what it's like to do the dirty part of vet care. The part that makes you feel alive."

"Well, I have plenty to do here to make you feel alive."

Conor chuckled. How like Christina to take him literally. "Let me check on Gold and give him a good walking and I'll be at your service. Are we good, Christina?"

"We are good."

She sounded like it, but he still couldn't be sure. He would just have to let time tell.

He spent the next hour seeing to Gold. Every once in a while, he caught sight of Christina swinging her hips as she listened to music and worked around the barn. She sang to the horses as well. He couldn't help but smile. Something he'd started to do more often since coming to America.

When it started to rain he brought Gold inside and put him in his stall. With that done he joined Christina in cleaning out stalls and replenishing hay. Every once in a while, she would remind him of something he'd missed. Still, he enjoyed the companionship, which he hadn't had in a long time.

Maybe now was the time to take a step forward. To move on with life. Couldn't he be friends with a woman and be true to Louisa at the same time? His family and friends, even Christina, had said it was time for him to move on. To have a second chance. Why shouldn't he start now? Christina had the kind heart to understand. He enjoyed her company. He couldn't think of anyone he'd rather spend time with.

He cleared his throat. It had been years since he'd done this. And after yesterday he wasn't sure she would agree. "Christina."

"Yes?" She turned to face him.

"I was wondering if you would like to go out to dinner this evening?"

Christina took a moment before she spoke. "I uh…don't think that's a good idea."

She had turned him down. He couldn't blame her after he'd stepped over the line. "Dinner. Nothing more."

"We shouldn't." She returned to using the pitch-fork to spread hay.

"Probably not. But I'm asking you to dinner between friends. Something to repay you for letting me stay here. It would also give me a night off from cooking." All of that was true but he still couldn't help but want more. He liked her. Couldn't seem to stay away from her.

She turned. "I'm sorry. I shouldn't have assumed."

"Not a problem." Apparently, his statement about not cooking caught her attention.

She confirmed that a second later. "I'm sorry. I should have thought about all the time you've spent in the kitchen. I imagine you'd like a night off. Thank you. I would like to go to dinner with you."

The knot of anxiousness between his shoulders eased. He had no idea until then he had been afraid she might say no. Tonight he would try to make up for mistreating her the previous evening.

That evening Conor waited in the kitchen. He forced himself not to pace. He was out of practice when it came to going out with a woman even if she was just a friend. He had not been out alone with a non-family member in years. But this wasn't a date, he reminded himself. Yet, it felt like a date.

Christina entered the kitchen dressed in a floral sleeveless dress with a V-neck that showed a hint of cleavage. The fabric hugged her breasts and fell in waves around her hips. Conor's mouth went dry. He forced a swallow. She was lovely like a new filly in the field.

Her auburn hair flowed around her shoulders. Pink touched her cheeks as she ran her hands down her dress. "Too much?"

"Not at all. But you look like we might have to call this a date."

Bright spots of red formed on her cheeks. "I don't get many chances to wear a dress, so I thought I'd wear one tonight. My mother would be proud of me."

"I'm glad you chose a dress." His gaze went to her legs, which were trim and muscular. Just perfect.

"Thank you."

"After you." He directed her toward the door.

As they exited through the back door of the house, Conor took a moment to appreciate the soft swing of her hips. *Not a date*, he repeated to himself. "I'll drive."

"You're one of those guys."

"I guess I am." He opened her door and waited for her to settle inside his truck.

"That was nice of you but not necessary."

"You work hard day in and day out. You deserve to be treated special on occasion." He went to the driver's seat and slipped behind the wheel. "You smell nice."

"Not of manure and horse?"

"I have no problem with the smell of barn, but this suits you better." He needed to slow down, or he'd be right back where he was yesterday if she would allow him to kiss her.

She clasped her hands in her lap. "Are you going to spend the entire evening embarrassing me?"

"I just might if you continue to blush."

She pushed at her cheeks. "I've always hated the way my emotions show on my face."

"I rather like knowing how you're feeling." He enjoyed knowing where he stood with her. Where was the guilt he had been feeling over the kiss? One look at Christina in a dress had him thinking of other things.

"Conor, this is a friendly outing."

"You're right. We're going to be two people enjoying each other's company over dinner." He turned out of the drive.

"Where're we going to do that?" she asked when he pulled onto the main highway.

"I went through Versailles the other day and did not have time to stop. I thought we would go there if you had no objection."

She hesitated a moment then said, "That sounds fine."

He glanced at her. "If you'd rather go elsewhere, we can do that."

She placed her hands back in her lap. "No, Versailles will be nice."

Twenty minutes later Christina walked beside him down the main street of the quaint town with its brick courthouse in the middle of an intersection. The 1940s storefronts had been maintained with care. Hot pink flowers hung in baskets from the lampposts. A rosy glow fell over everything as the sun lowered.

Christina had covered her bare shoulders with a sweater while he enjoyed the warmth with his sleeves rolled up his forearms. He resisted putting his hand at her back. Yet, he remained close but not touching. He had already gotten in over his head where she was concerned. Was it from his forced proximity to Christina or was the attraction that strong?

He remained conflicted over his feelings for her, yet he couldn't keep his distance from Christina.

Christina, to his knowledge, had never made a movement he could have called a stroll. Tonight was no different. It was as if she were a horse pulling on the reins to go faster.

"If we don't hurry up, there might not be any tables. Then we'll have a wait."

"I'm enjoying the stroll with you." He wanted

to spend as much time as he could with her. That way maybe he would better understand this temptation between them.

"What?"

"It's about slowing down and appreciating life. Something you find difficult, I know." He had learned to do that. Having lost someone special, he knew about appreciating time. He would be leaving Christina in another week and a half, and he wanted what time he could have with her. His footsteps faltered. That idea hit him like a kick in the chest. Since when did spending time with Christina become so important?

What about Louisa? Christina was right. Louisa would want his happiness.

From what he understood the week of the Derby would be busy. He would be lucky if he saw Christina at all. Sadness fell over him. They didn't have much time to explore what was between them. Did she want to?

"What makes you think you know me that well?" She sounded irritated by the idea he might see something she didn't want others to see.

"Because I've watched you over the last week and I've gotten to know you pretty well."

Her eyes widened.

Conor took her elbow to gently move her out of the way of a group walking toward them. "Now, where would you like to eat? It can be anywhere."

"There's a nice restaurant right down here on the corner." She pointed ahead of them.

"Then that is where we will go." It was the first time he'd used a firm tone with her, but he was not going to let her change her mind. The woman really did need to take time to enjoy life some.

She huffed. "You're not the boss of me."

"No, I am not, but you are my dinner date...uh friend. I like them to have a smile on their face when they eat with me."

"Says the man that showed up at my farm a little more than a week ago looking like a thundercloud."

He smiled. "My brother and sister said something like that before I left."

She patted his arm. "With good reason."

They paused in front of the restaurant. It had matching front windows on either side of the dark wooden door. On both the windows was etched the word *Thoroughbred*. Above that was the figure of a horse stretched out in a run. In the corners were filigrees. Light from inside spilled out onto the sidewalk.

He held the door open for Christina. She balked at entering. "Maybe we should go somewhere else."

Was this about the same thing that had her hesitating on the ride over? Did it have to do with him or had she seen someone she didn't want to face?

Her expression said she might be uncomfortable with the idea but she quickly recovered.

She inhaled a breath as if bracing herself before she stepped inside.

"Hey, Christina," the woman behind the hostess desk said.

"Hello, Jean. Do you have a booth available?" Christina asked with a note of forced brightness.

The woman smiled. "Sure. Just take a spot wherever you like."

"Thanks." Christina didn't wait on him but headed toward the far side of the room away from the door and traffic. She slid into a booth constructed to look like a barn stall as if relieved to get there.

Who was she hiding from?

He ran a hand down the smooth pieces of wood that made their booth. "These look like the real thing."

"They are from an old barn that was torn down near mine." She looked at the table.

"I like it. This old-world work reminds me of home." He took a seat on the red cushion and settled in front of her. "This is an interesting place."

A teenage waitress stood at the end of the table and handed them a plastic-covered menu.

During their meal a number of people casually spoke to Christina as they were coming to their tables or leaving. Each time she acted unsure when they approached then pleasantly surprised at their greeting. Just what was her problem?

Conor settled back in the booth watching Christina. "Apparently, you are well-known around here."

Her eyes flickered up to meet his look. "Yes. I grew up in Versailles. But that can have its disadvantages."

Those would be...? "True, but I bet it can have advantages as well."

She crossed her arms on the table, looking directly at him. "Have you lived in the same spot most of your life?"

"Yes."

"Then you must know what it's like for everyone to know your business good or bad."

"I do." His home was a place where everyone knew his pain. Like that his wife didn't love him enough to stay alive. That his father cheated on his mother. These memories walked daily with him. The expressions on townsfolk's faces held pity. The ones he hid from. Yet, it was home. "I've lived in the same village my entire life except for when I left for school." He needed a change in subject. "This is the kind of place that reminds me of a pub back home. But only quieter."

She looked beyond them. "It'll get noisier later. I've never been to a pub."

"Never? Our pubs are where the whole community hangs out. You couldn't live in Ireland without finding your pub. Have you ever thought about visiting Ireland?"

"No, but I've always wanted to travel. With the farm and horses to care for it's hard to get away. Maybe one day."

He turned the water glass in his hands. "I guess it doesn't ever let up. If you do come let me know and I'll show you around."

"I doubt that will happen any time soon. I'm trying to build up a business." Her voice held a wistful note.

"Why are you trying to do that instead of just having your regular practice? I would think it would be enough."

Christina let out a breath slowly. She leaned back against the booth. "Well, I sort of just fell into it. My ex-partner had the idea. When he left, I just couldn't close it down."

"But that doesn't mean that you don't need a life outside of here." He looked around the room.

She leaned back and pinned him with a look. "Is this the man whose family had to force him to come to America?"

The woman didn't mind hitting hard. "You have a point."

She smiled. For once that evening, she looked relaxed. "Tell me about Ireland."

He smiled. "I think you would like it. It reminds

me very much of Kentucky with its rolling hills and green grass. The people are friendly. We've got stone walls, where you've got all these wooden fences, but we love our horses. We've got cooler temperatures."

She grinned. "You love the place as much as I love here."

"I do love it." But oddly, he hadn't missed it like he had when he had first arrived.

Christina stepped out of the restaurant to the streetlights burning. She had enjoyed her dinner with Conor more than she'd imagined. She had gone to extra trouble dressing and his reaction had been worth the trouble. Then to have his complete attention focused on her had heated her skin. More than once her heart had skipped a beat when his hand had brushed hers as they walked down the street or reached for something at the same time at the table.

She had to stop herself a couple of times from staring at his lips.

The only negative of the evening had been her reaction to going into the Thoroughbred. She had misjudged her strength in being able to handle returning. It had been a regular place for her and Nelson to join friends. Those who disappeared when she had been in trouble.

She'd had a choice to admit that to Conor or make herself hold her head high. The latter won. Being with Conor gave her extra reassurance. She was with a handsome man who would support and protect her.

How did she know that? Because he'd done nothing but show that since she had met him. She believed he was a good man. But hadn't her judgment been off before?

"A few people I've met have mentioned there is a small racetrack around here and that there is racing tonight. Would you like to go?"

She couldn't go there. The urge to shake her head wildly filled her but she didn't do it. What would she do if someone said the wrong thing in front of Conor? She would die. "I don't know. I should really get home and make sure the horses are settled for the night."

"I can help you do that when we get back. I'd like to see how a race is run before the Derby."

She quickly released a sigh. "Okay, we can go for a few races."

In the car he said, "How about giving me directions."

"Turn left. It's only a few miles out of town. There's a large sign on the highway." They were walking toward the racetrack when she said, "These are the horses that didn't make the Kentucky Derby cut or probably never would but the locals coming here have fun watching the horses race. It's also a good place for the jockeys to learn and get experience."

She led Conor to the entrance where a woman sat at a portable table with a metal box at hand.

"Hi, Christina. We haven't seen you around in a while." The woman took the money Conor offered her.

Christina stiffened. She was surprised Emily sounded genuinely glad to see her. "Hello. It's nice to see you again."

They continued toward the stands.

Conor walked beside her. "Apparently, they know you here, too."

"Yes, I used to work here on the weekends." She led the way to a seat in one of the two metal bleachers going to the second row from the top. "I like to see. I love the horses, but I also love coming to the races. I've always enjoyed the small track. Sometimes I think they're more fun than the big races. Here you can really see the horses. And the crowd likes watching them instead of being seen themselves."

Conor sat beside her just out of touching distance but close enough she could feel his heat. Her skin tingled with his nearness.

"Tell me about your races. I understand they're different from ours."

"There will be several races tonight but lots more on Derby Day, including the Derby. The horses run ten furlongs, or about one and a half US miles. Only three-year-olds run on a dirt track. These tonight will be very similar to those at Churchill Downs on Kentucky Derby Day."

"Do you bet much?" Conor looked toward the betting boxes.

"Almost never. When I'm working they don't allow it. Therefore, I make it a practice not to do it." She had already had a close call with the law once and she wouldn't give the racing commission a reason to question her behavior again.

"Christina." A woman called her from the aisle of the stands.

"Hi, Lucy. It's good to see you."

"You, too. How have you been?" Lucy sounded sincere.

"Just working a lot. How about you?" Lucy had been her friend.

"Busy, too. I was sorry about what happened to you. I haven't had a chance to tell you that. I should've been a better friend and believed in you." Lucy's look didn't waver.

"Thank you for saying that." Even now it was nice.

Lucy smiled. "Well, I better get back to work. I hope you come around more often."

Christina said to Conor, "Sorry I didn't introduce you. Lucy runs this racetrack."

* * *

She had been Christina's best friend, but Nelson's lies had fractured that as well. That, Christina didn't plan to dwell on. She'd been enjoying herself tonight. Conor had been a wonderful dinner companion. She didn't want to talk about the past and ruin the time they had together.

Conor looked out toward the track. "This reminds me of our local course at home."

Christina followed his gaze. There weren't any barns just horse trailers hitched to big trucks in a large lot off in a distance. The track was grass. It had been cut and trimmed. There was a well-used horse gate stationed across the track.

"Really? How is that? I understand your races are a cross between a steeplechase and a regular race."

"Some of them are." He leaned forward, resting his elbows on his knees.

"I have seen horses jumping on TV but I have no idea what happens in your races. I bet it makes for an interesting experience with the combo of jumping and running."

"It does." Conor intensely watched the activity in the area. He was a man who looked at the details.

"That certainly adds an element of danger to the event."

"It does but it also adds to the challenge." He commented without looking at her.

"I could see your point there. It sounds rather exciting." She would like to see one someday.

"We like to think so. We don't have such a large spectator area as Churchill Downs. Our seating is simpler. When the horses come up to the starting line people pour to the outside, and when they're not racing, they go inside under the stands to the bar and to place their bets."

"That's interesting. Our attendees pretty much live in the stands. You'll be amazed on Derby Day the number of people there. The pomp and circumstance involved, the traditions."

He looked at her and grinned. "I look forward to it. And Gold winning his race."

She had to admit she would be pulling for the horse. "Wouldn't that be exciting? You'll enjoy the Oaks race on Friday when the three-year-old fillies run. The stands will be almost as full and it's all day as well."

"But I guess you'll be busy."

Conor sounded disappointed she wouldn't be sharing it with him. It was nice to have someone want to share her company.

The announcer called over the microphone. "The horses are in the gate." Seconds later he announced, "And they're off."

The crowd stood. The horses ran around the first curve.

Christina went up on her toes in an effort to see better. When she wobbled, she grasped Conor's forearm so she wouldn't fall. His arm went around her waist when she climbed on the bench to stand on it. She spoke to Conor without looking. "Sorry, I can't see. I do miss having a large television screen like they have at Churchill Downs. I can't tell how they're doing on the backside."

Even in the distance the thunder of the horses' hooves could be heard. The horses came around the second back turn.

Christina stretched to see. She registered the tightening of Conor's arm. He wouldn't let her fall.

The crowd grew louder along with the pounding of hooves. The horses made the front curve and entered the part of the track in front of them. Unable to help herself Christina started jumping.

"They're coming down the stretch," the announcer said.

The crowd cheered as the horses thundered across the finish line.

Christina whooped then threw her arms around Conor's neck. His arms wrapped around her waist and held her. He grinned up at her with amazement sparkling in his eyes. Reality struck her. She pushed away from him and stepped down from the bench, pushing her dress into place. "I'm sorry. I should've warned you I get carried away."

He chuckled. "I have no problem with that. My arm may be bruised in the morning but it will have been worth it."

What must he think? After yesterday's kiss and her reaction and then she throws herself at him. She needed to put some distance between them. She patted his upper arm. "I'm sorry. I didn't mean to hurt you."

His arm squeezed her closer. "I enjoyed it. It's nice to see you happy."

During the next race she tried to restrain herself but didn't manage to do much better than she had earlier. Conor grinned then offered his hand to help her up on the bleacher and supported her once more. She looked forward to his protection with each race. Apparently, she wouldn't be successful in keeping her distance.

In the last race the horses rounded the last turn toward the finish line, one horse bumped another then another stumbled into another before two horses went down.

Christina held her breath. She didn't see something like this often, but she had seen it before. It didn't end up well.

The jockeys moved quickly to get away from the horses. Jockeys still in the saddle continued for the finish line. The fallen horses kicked to stand while the racetrack staff ran onto the field. One staff member ran out from the sideline and grabbed the reins and tugged the most active horse's head, encouraging him to his feet. With one swift movement he stood.

The other horse lay on the ground, unmoving. In less than ten seconds a large blue screen had been placed so that the crowd couldn't see what was happening.

CHAPTER FIVE

CONOR ALWAYS HATED to see a screen go up. It didn't bode well for the horse.

Christina brushed behind him on her way down the bench toward the steps.

"Hey, where are you going?"

She pointed down.

It was then he saw her friend Lucy with her hand in the air, waving Christina down to the track. Conor didn't hesitate to follow. He made his way around people who had stepped out into the stairs.

He joined the women just as Lucy said with panic in her voice, "I could use your help."

She didn't wait on Christina to answer.

She followed, keeping pace behind Lucy. Conor was behind Christina as they hurried toward where the accident had happened.

Lucy said over her shoulder as they moved. "Our vet for tonight had an emergency and just left. The replacement is on the way but isn't here yet. It's a blessing you were here tonight."

They reached the track. There they went through a gate and loped across the grass track to where the screen stood. The need for it meant the horse would probably be put down. Unfortunately, accidents were part of the sport. An ugly part.

He followed Christina behind the screen to a scene he had expected. Christina went immediately to her knees beside the horse. She patted his neck. Fear filled the animal's large dark eyes. "Easy, boy, help is here. Easy."

Conor dropped down beside her. He ran his hand over the horse's back legs. Christina did the same on the front.

"I can't find a break here." She continued her examination.

Conor finished his. "I don't find one here, either."

Christina patted the horse's neck once again. She moved her hand over the horse's shoulder and along his back. "No obvious broken bones. Let's see if we can get him up on his feet."

"Let me get around on the other side so I can help push him." Conor moved opposite her.

Christina took the reins and stood. The horse kicked his feet. "Okay, boy, let's see you stand."

A couple of grooms joined Conor. "We're ready."

"Easy, boy. Slow and easy." She tugged on the

reins. Conor pushed the horse. The men beside him did as well.

All the while, Christina continued to talk to the scared animal. Suddenly, the horse kicked and rolled and came to its feet. Conor stepped back to where he could see the horse's movements. He did not see a problem.

"Conor, do you see any issues?"

"No. He looks good to me."

"We'll give him a moment for his head to quit spinning." She stroked the nose of the horse, who settled before their eyes. "Now we're going take a little walk around," Christina said to the horse then led him in a circle.

While she did, Conor watched every movement the horse made for a limp or hesitation. With the next slow turn he saw it. "There it is. Right fore-leg."

Christina stopped the horse. She handed the reins to a groom. "Slow walk."

The groom nudged the horse forward.

She stood beside Conor. "I see it now. Let's get it wrapped up and secure. Then he'll need X-rays."

An older man ran around the screen. He came to an abrupt stop. He demanded as he looked at Christina, "What are you doing here?"

Christina stiffened beside Conor. Who was this guy? Why was he speaking to Christina that way?

"Lucy asked me to help."

"We don't want you here. The racetrack doesn't need any more trouble because of you." He glared at her.

"I understand how you feel about that, but that's not the case here. I was vindicated."

Vindicated? What was she talking about? Conor stepped closer.

She glanced at him. He stopped. "Doctor Victor," she said to the man, "I'll go but first you need to know that the horse has an issue with the right front foreleg. It is barely detectable to the eye. X-rays will be required."

"I can handle this. Thank you." Dr. Victor turned his back to her.

Conor felt her tremble. "Christina, I think we're done here."

Her attention didn't leave the horse and the movements of the man, but she didn't argue. Conor took her hand and led her away. They walked out the gate to the parking lot. At the car she got in without saying a word.

He didn't start the car. Instead, he turned to face her. "You want to tell me what that was all about?"

"Not really."

He watched her a moment then nodded and started the car. He knew from experience that if someone didn't want to talk, he couldn't make them. He had been the same with his siblings. He pulled out of the gravel parking lot.

"You aren't going to try any harder than that to find out?" She almost sounded disappointed.

Conor glanced at her. "You'll tell me when you are ready."

"I guess you deserve some explanation."

She made it sound as if she wasn't convinced he did.

"It's not a nice story."

He looked at her again. "I've heard ugly stories before."

She started slowly. "About a year and a half ago all those people who spoke to me this evening had stopped doing so."

"Why?" That had to have hurt her.

"Because they thought I had been stealing and selling drugs. In fact, I almost lost my license. If I hadn't had the paperwork to prove I had followed the rules, I would have had the racing commission on me. Doctor Victor, the man who just came up, was on the board then. I came closer than I ever want to again to losing my license."

Now Conor understood the interaction between them. "So what happened?"

"My ex. Who lived with me for four years. Who had access to my medicines. Who said he loved me but pointed his finger at me when the authorities started asking questions."

Conor wanted to punch something on her behalf. The pain in her voice made her ex a prime candidate. "What was he doing with the drugs? Taking them or selling them?"

"Both. To make matters worse he gambled on the horses, which is a no-no and was stealing to pay his gambling debt. What made it worse was I thought he loved me. That we were going to get married and start a family."

He winced. Marriage and family. What he had once wanted. But no longer. "I get why working at the Derby is so important to you now. It's your way of proving you aren't the person everyone said you were."

"Yeah. Regaining my good reputation is important to me in general but to my work with horses as well. People need to trust me. Horse racing is a small world. And to start a new business in it is difficult. What made me really mad was I was too stupid to see what he was doing. I trusted him. I can't trust my judgment anymore."

"I can see why. I'm sorry that happened to you." She had endured more than she should have.

"Things are better now. Even as hard as it was to walk into the racetrack tonight, it felt good to have people speak to me. I'm starting to rebuild my reputation."

"I haven't known you long but I think you are doing just fine. It takes time." He certainly knew that well. Three years later he had just started working through his wife's death. He took Christina's hand and squeezed it. "I know I would have missed out if I'd never met you."

Christina appreciated his warmth. Conor's words felt like a hot drink flowing through her. He made her want to believe him. She looked at his handsome profile. He was a nice man.

Conor continued to hold her hand. Gently, he rubbed the top of it with the pad of his thumb. "You have to be true to yourself. You know you are honest. You can't carry others' mistakes as yours."

"To say that is one thing. To live it is another." She relaxed in her seat, appreciating his reassurance.

"You shouldn't have had to deal with all that."

"I was the one that should have noticed or maybe subconsciously I did, but didn't want to know."

"Nor can you be perfect and all-knowing."

Her mother had certainly expected that of her. Do it better, be better, do it just so. Christina hadn't ever felt like she measured up. The thing with Nelson just proved she never would. Here Conor was telling her that she didn't have to do more than be herself. "Thanks for the vote of confidence. You have no idea what the means to me."

"Now I understand why you are so particular about counting your medicine cabinet."

"Yeah, I keep a strict count now. I take no chances." She wouldn't be put in a position of explaining herself again.

"Being super vigilant isn't a bad thing. What isn't healthy is obsessing over it. It's past time for you to move forward."

"You don't think I already know all of that?" Her words had a sharp note to them.

"Oh, I'm sure you do but you need to be reminded of it." He grinned.

They remained in their own thoughts the rest of the way home.

Conor pulled behind the house and shut off the car.

"I need to check on the horses." She was out of the car and at the back door before he caught up with her.

He called, "Hey, wait a minute. You're not running from me, are you?"

She looked at him, her eyes watering. "I don't know. Maybe I'm running from myself."

He cupped her cheek. "You have no reason to be afraid of me. I'm your friend, Christina. You can trust me."

And she knew she could. Christina loved the feel of Conor's skin touching hers. She wanted to lean in to his warmth and reassurance. But if she did, it would soon be gone. She couldn't let herself need it. "I know. Come on, we need to see about the horses."

He sighed, letting his fingertips trail across her cheek. "Yes, the horses."

It had rained while they were gone. They changed into their rubber boots and walked out to the barn. Conor went to see about Gold while she went through her nightly routine. He waited at the barn doors when he finished.

Christina flipped off the inside lights. Conor helped her close and secure the doors. The outside security light formed a subdued glow around them.

"You know, you're doing yourself a disservice. You have to know how amazing you are."

"Thank you. That was a nice thing to say. I'm the one who should be thanking you for your support tonight. For a moment there I thought you were gonna pick up a sword and shield. Maybe I should move away from here so I can leave it all behind."

"Take my word for it, it doesn't work like that. I've left a country behind and it is still here with me."

"You miss your wife, don't you?" Christina couldn't help asking.

"Every day."

What would it be like to be loved so completely? To know that another person had your back no matter what. That you were enough for them.

"I can say that it eases. But you do carry it

around with you all the time. Coming here helped.
I didn't think it would, but it did."

"I'm glad. I just don't want to forget what can
happen if you trust too much and mess up again."

Christina stopped, watching him. She had been
so embarrassed in front of him tonight but instead
of turning against her he'd stepped forward as if
he would fight for her honor. More than that, he
had listened, really listened to her. For that, she
could kiss him. "Thank you for being a nice guy."

Placing her hands on his shoulders, she went up
on her toes and gave him a soft kiss on the lips.
She stepped back.

Conor looked at her a second before he pulled
her against him. His lips found hers. She leaned
in to him. As his lips applied more pressure, his
hands moved over her back. Her muscles rippled
under Conor's touch just as the horses did when
she caressed them. The man had a tender touch.

His mouth released hers. Placing his forehead
against hers, he whispered in a reverent tone,
"Christina."

She liked the way her name rolled over his lips
in his Irish brogue.

"Yes?" The word came out breathy.

"I know after yesterday I don't have the right
to say this but I want you. Something I've not felt
in a long time."

"Kiss me."

* * *

Conor didn't make her ask twice. She didn't have to ask. He gathered her into his arms and pulled her firmly against him. His mouth slanted across hers with more pressure than before. Her arms wrapped around his neck as she leaned closer. His hands circled and tightened on her waist.

"I don't know what you've done to me." He kissed her temple. "I've been in this fog for months, years, and all of a sudden around you it's sunshine." His mouth moved over her smooth skin to her ear. Taking her earlobe, he gave it a gentle tug. Christina made a soft noise of pleasure in her throat. The sound fed his desire. She tilted her head, giving him better access. He kissed along the long column of her neck.

This time she purred. Lifting her shoulder, she kept his lips against her skin. She ran her hands across his chest then up and over his shoulders as if memorizing his body with the tips of her fingers.

His mouth found hers once more. He kissed her deeply. She returned his kisses with enthusiasm. Conor loved her passion. He tightened his hold. She pressed against him as she ran her fingers through his hair. If he'd known Christina could kiss like this he would have kissed her sooner. She made his body pulsate. Like a horse waiting for the starting gate to open.

At this rate she'd drive him crazy. He had said he didn't want this. But he did with every fiber of his being. He feared he might be taking advantage of the fact Christina was there and available. No, everything about Christina urged him on. Pulled him to her. He was powerless to turn away. Her special appeal was part of who she was. A tiny feminine woman wrapped in dirty jeans and boots had awakened a craving only she could satisfy.

This lusty fervor for Christina he liked too much. He found her plush mouth again.

A drop of rain hit him on the forehead. It didn't dampen his attention or desire. He continued to sip on her lips. The rain turned steady and he broke away. "I need to get you out of the rain before we're both soaked."

"Like you were yesterday." She giggled.

He kissed her hard. "I will get you for that." He reached around her and opened the door. "In you go."

"Promises, promises." Christina stepped into the kitchen where the only light came from the hall. She moved to the kitchen counter. Her back remained to him.

He sucked in a breath until his chest hurt. "About promises."

She looked over her shoulder. "Don't worry. I don't expect any. I know you can't give them."

Conor released the air but found the pain had

not eased. "I don't want you hurt. I will be leaving after the Derby."

"I know it."

Had Christina started second-guessing what had been happening between them? Maybe that was just as well. He wanted her but what she wanted and deserved he couldn't offer. For so many reasons. The least being he lived thousands of miles away.

"Coffee? Tea?"

What he wanted was her back in his arms, but he wouldn't say that.

The rain had turned heavy and lightning shot across the sky, making the dark room bright for a moment.

Christina jerked.

He made a step toward her.

"I'm fine. The thunder always gets me, but I love the rain. Which is good because I need to go check on the horses. That lightning will not have made them happy."

"Let me do that. I need to check on Gold. He can get wild-eyed quickly."

She started toward the door. "You don't have to do that."

He gave her an earnest look, his gaze fixed with hers. "Let me do something nice for you."

She stopped. "Okay. Thank you."

Walking to the door he said, "I enjoyed my

evening with you more than I have anything in a long time. Thank you."

"Same for me."

Before he closed the door behind him he said, "Good night, Christina."

"'Night," she said so low he almost missed it.

Conor hunched his shoulders against the cool wind and rain as he hurried across the yard to the barn. He was grateful for the weather for bringing the temperature of his body back in line after kissing Christina.

The horses whinnied and shifted as he walked down the hall, checking inside each stall. Satisfied that all was well, he returned to the house. Inside again he turned off the porch light, leaving darkness. The hall light no longer glowed. He removed his boots and padded in socked feet to the bath.

"Are they okay?" Christina stood in her bedroom doorway with the light from her bedside table behind her. She wore a short, flimsy nightgown that the glow made transparent.

Conor swallowed. Those breasts he had been treated to a hint of days before were visible through the fabric. His blood flowed faster. His length had hardened. Why hadn't she gone in her room and stayed? He was torn between being glad she'd been waiting on him and fearing he couldn't stop himself from reaching for her.

Is this what his father faced when he'd been

unfaithful to his wife and family? No, this wasn't the same. Louisa was gone by her own choice. He shoved his hands into his pockets. Even now his body vibrated with the desire to taste her, touch her, experience her. "I didn't mean to disturb you."

Her gaze met his, held.

The air turned thick. The rain pounded on the roof as his heart hammered in his chest. This was one of those crossroads in life where if he said or did the wrong thing he would live to regret it. So he waited.

"Uh…about a while ago… I…" She ran her fingers through her hair.

That made her nightgown flow around her. He could see the lines of her sweet body. "You… what? Tell me, Christina. What do you want?"

"I want you."

His heart kicked into overdrive. "I'm right here. All you have to do is reach out."

She took his hand, turned and led him into her room. Stopping beside her bed, she said, "Make love to me, Conor."

"Are you sure that's what you want?" He wanted no regrets for either of them in the morning.

"Yes."

"No promises. No tomorrows. Just now. Just feeling. I haven't felt in so long. I want to again. With you." He needed that so desperately, he hurt with it.

She looked toward the bed and nodded. He cupped her face in both his hands. Her eyes watched him, wide and unsure.

"We are going to take this slow and easy." He lightly brushed her mouth with his lips.

Her hands came to his shoulders.

He continued to kiss and caress and tease her mouth until her fingers bit into his muscles. His hands didn't leave her face as he deepened his kisses. He reveled in the soft, erotic sounds Christina made.

She returned his kisses. He ran his tongue along the seam of her lips and she opened for him. Greeted him. At first, she hesitated but with one brush of his tongue she joined him in the dance. Even leading at times.

His manhood stood thick and ready. He wanted her now but giving her pleasure won out. Too much had been taken from her. She deserved to feel how special she was.

Her hands moved down over his chest, bunching in his shirt as his tongue stroked hers.

The fingers of one hand traveled along her neck, brushing the tender spot behind her ear then moving across the ridge of her shoulders to cup her bare arm. The other hand followed its lead. He ran the pads of his thumbs beneath the material of her nothing pajamas to touch the swells of her breasts.

Christina shivered. Her hands moved to his waist. She pressed into him.

His manhood throbbed, needing release. He swept a finger over her nipple. A burst of heat flashed through him when he found it stiff and tall, begging for his attention. His mouth left hers to travel over her cheek, down her neck. Cupping her breast, he lifted it and placed his mouth over it. Even with the material barring her from his mouth he continued to suck and tug at the tiny expressive part of her body. He looked at the material sealed over her beauty.

His fingertips touched her thighs. She trembled. His hand crawled under the short gown and over her hips, gathering the material as he went.

Christina stood still, only the rise and fall of her chest visible. Occasionally, there was a lurch and jump in her breathing. He revealed her breasts as if removing a silk drape from a famous piece of artwork with great anticipation and reverence. Unable to stand it any longer, he placed his mouth over a nipple.

Her breath hissed through her lips. Her fingers threaded through his hair, caressing him as he ran his tongue around her nipple to pull and suck. He held her at the waist with one hand and moved to the other breast, giving it the same administrations. His other hand found the edge of her panties and teased the skin there.

Christina quivered, her hands now resting on his shoulders. He left her breasts to kiss the hollow between them. From there his mouth kissed a line to the band of her bikini panties.

"Conor, it's my turn." Her words drifted around them, they were so soft. She tugged him upward.

He stood, his hands still exploring as he went.

The moment he reached his height, Christina's hands went to the top of his shirt. Their mouths met once again. All the while, her fingers worked the buttons from their holes. She pushed the material over his shoulders. He released her long enough for the shirt to drop to the floor. Before he could touch her again, she placed her palms on his chest, keeping the space between them.

Her fingertips dragged over his skin, sending tingling heat throughout his body. His nerves bunched and released as she went. He reached for her, and she moved his hands away.

"I'm not done admiring you. I've been thinking about nothing but touching you since I ran into you in the hall the other morning."

"That was days ago."

"Uh-huh." She kissed him just over his heart.

She had covered up that need well. "You never let on."

"I couldn't." She looked at him and grinned. "I didn't want to look like I was taking advantage of a houseguest."

This time he didn't let her stop him. He took her in his arms. "Take advantage of me any time you wish."

Christina giggled.

"I love that sound."

"What?" She gave him a perplexed look.

He grinned. "The sound of you happy."

Her hands came up his chest and circled his neck. "It's nice to feel that for a change."

He gave her a couple of quick kisses. "You should have that all the time. Now, enough of the talk. I want to explore you more." His hands found the hem of her gown and pulled it over her head. He let it go to land on his shirt.

Cupping her breasts in his hands, he kissed one then the other. He backed her to the bed, laying her on it, then joined her.

She pulled him to her. Pressed against her smooth skin, he found utopia. He rolled to his side and placed his hand on her stomach. Her skin rippled. His manhood twitched with need. Leisurely, far more so than he felt, he moved his hand down to her pink panties, slipping a finger beneath. His reward was the hitch in her breathing.

"These need to come off," he said before he kissed the dip where her neck met her shoulder.

She pushed at the panties then wiggled until she could kick them off her foot.

It might have been the sexiest thing he'd ever

seen. The knowledge that what had been revealed would be his made him hotter than ever.

Christina pulled him to her, giving him a searing kiss. Her hands flowed over his back, causing his muscles to ripple.

His hand caressed the silkiness of her inner thigh before traveling to where her legs joined. He brushed his palm over her curls then went in search of her center. He found it warm and wet. Waiting for him. Slipping a finger inside her, he earned her whimper. Her hips flexed in greeting. Behind the zipper of his pants, his manhood ached for relief.

He continued moving his finger inside and out.

Christina lifted her hips, stiffened and keened her pleasure before she shivered and relaxed on the bed.

Satisfaction filled him. He wanted her to have the best pleasure he could provide. Conor kissed her lips, cheeks, eyes, tenderly giving her the attention and care she deserved all while holding her close.

Moments went by then she brushed his hair back from his forehead and looked into his eyes. "It's past time to take off your pants. I want you. All of you."

CHAPTER SIX

CHRISTINA COULDN'T BELIEVE what had just happened to her. She still basked in the waves of pleasure from her release. This was a new experience. Sex had never been as powerful between her and Nelson. And Conor hadn't even been inside her. Doubts rushed in. Would she be enough for Conor?

He stood and started removing his clothes.

She watched as his hands went to his belt. "Would you like us to get under the covers?"

His gaze remained on her. "I would like whatever you do."

"I didn't plan on this or I would have put on clean sheets."

"I don't care about the sheets," he all but growled. He removed his wallet and placed it on the bedside table then lowered his zipper.

Her mouth gaped at the size of him. She watched in anticipation as he pushed his pants down. Her mouth went dry. "Do you have a condom?"

He grinned. "I do."

"Are you always so prepared?"

"I try to be." He looked directly at her. "It has been a long time for me."

"Me, too." But he was worth waiting for.

When he shoved his boxers to the floor she sucked in a breath. He was all beautiful male.

He stepped closer to the bed. "Why all the sudden chatter?"

"I'm nervous."

"What do you have to be nervous about? You're beautiful and desirable." He pushed her hair off her cheek and cupped it.

"You're just saying that so I don't run off." The temptation to get under the covers grew.

His knee rested on the bed as he looked over at her.

She looked away. "I don't want to disappoint you."

"Just what makes you think you would disappoint me?"

"It's been a long time for me. I may not be any good." She just couldn't fail this man who had just given her so much pleasure. If this would be their one and only time, she wanted Conor to remember her.

He looked into her eyes. "I can't imagine how that would ever be true."

"More than one person has told me I don't measure up. Or I could be better." Her mother. Nelson. "It makes you doubt yourself."

He gave her an incredulous look. "At having sex?"

"At anything. My mother told me that. My ex stole from me, and I had no idea. This may be another area where I'm lacking."

"I tell you what. We will go slow. It's been a while for me also. We are in this together unless you would like me to leave."

"No. Please don't go."

"I'm not going anywhere unless you tell me to." He gave her the same gentling caress along her back she'd seen him give a fearful animal. He spoke her language. "I don't see how you could disappointment me in bed or out—ever."

He stopped her next words by sealing her mouth with his.

She ran her hands over his ribs, enjoying the firm male feel of Conor, to the expanse of his back. His hand cupped her breast, kneading it, teasing it. Her center tingled, and heated. His manhood pressed against her stomach. She wiggled.

Conor broke the kiss. "You keep that up and I'll be done before we get started."

She teased him with the movement of her hips. "I thought we had started some time ago."

Conor rolled away and picked up his wallet.

He removed a little square package, making short order of opening it and covering himself. Returning to her, he took her into his arms again, giving her gentle kisses that had her wanting more and more.

She opened her legs in welcome. He settled between them. Rising over her on his hands, he entered her. She closed her eyes focusing on each movement of him inside her. He filled her and stopped.

Daring a look, she found Conor's face tight in concentration as if he were absorbing every second of their joining.

He pulled back, making her fear he would leave her, before he returned. His movements continued with deliberation until he had her urging him forward while she clutched the sheets and her legs trembled in desperation.

Heat coiled low in her, tightened, folded on itself and burst. She was flung into the air and slowly drifted on pleasure. In a dreamlike trance she drifted back to reality.

Conor increased his pace, pumping into her like his life depended on it.

She wrapped her legs around his waist, pulling him closer. He groaned and sank into her with force. She joined him in the push-pull moments. Conor stiffened, holding himself steady and roared his release.

If she wanted confirmation of her ability to please a man, she had it.

He came down, covering her with his hard, warm and relaxed body.

When he became too heavy she squirmed, and Conor rolled to his back. He pulled her close as their breathing returned to normal.

Conor listened to the rain with Christina's soft, warm body snuggled against his. Disappointment hadn't happened. Christina had been everything he'd ever dreamed a lover should be. He had missed this type of connection with a female. He'd not allowed himself the pleasure of a woman in so long. And to have this special big-hearted female next to him made his heart open again.

Christina sighed heavily.

He gave her a gentle squeeze. "Am I boring you?"

"No, I was just trying to figure out if I should ask you something or not." She ran her hand across his waist.

"You can ask me anything. If you are planning to ask if you were a disappointment then don't bother. You should have been able to tell I thought you were amazing."

"Thanks for that." She turned so he could see her face. "It wasn't that. I wondered if you would tell me about your wife. What happened to her."

Conor tensed. He didn't talk about that. The real story hurt too much. Christina waited. "You want to talk about her now?"

"Yes. I want to know about the woman so special you spent years in sadness after losing her."

It hadn't been just her. But he couldn't even tell Christina about the baby. The pain was still too great. He'd never said the words to anyone. Not even his brother or sister. He didn't want Christina knowing what he had done to his child. He wasn't sure he ever could tell her. He feared he would double over in agony just as he had when the doctor had said, "I'm sorry about the baby as well."

Conor cleared his throat and gathered his fortitude. Christina deserved his trust. She had earned it. "We had a little house in the village. A place we all grew up. Family and friends, and a busy social life. My practice was thriving. But one thing was missing. She always laughed and said she was the perfect childbearing wife. She would pat her hips."

Christina moved so she could look down at him. "Do you have children?"

He almost left the bed, but he forced himself to stay where he was. He would get through this. "No. It wasn't from the lack of trying. Sadly, we never conceived. Even after going through the medical system. As time went by, she became mired in sadness over the situation. Not emotionally strong to begin with, she took our problems particularly hard. She slowly disappeared on me. Becoming a hull of who she was because she wanted children so desperately. It became an issue in our marriage."

Christina's eyes turned sad with concern. "I shouldn't have asked you, but I understand her wanting them so much."

He could imagine Christina as a mother. She would be a wonderful one. Yet, their time together wasn't about creating a family. It was only for the here and now. Still, something nudged him to talk to her. To have her understand what happened between him and Louisa. "We had a horrible fight. I told her I couldn't live like we were anymore. Something had to change. Because of me, the ugly things I said, she went out and saw to it by driving her car into a rock wall."

"Oh, Conor. How awful. I'm so sorry." Christina placed her head on his shoulder and wrapped her arms around his waist and hugged him tightly. "It wasn't your fault."

He wasn't convinced that was true. He'd said all those horrible things to Louisa, yet she'd carried the baby he had given her. Then killed herself because she didn't know. How could that not be his fault? For years he had lived with the conviction he should have known, should have seen the damage he had been doing to Louisa. Why hadn't he seen the mental state she was in? He should have noticed.

He'd helped to create it. Just by saying the words *I will leave you.* He hadn't meant them. He'd made a vow to stay with her in good times and bad. He had been and still was determined he would be better than his father. Threatening to leave hadn't been the answer.

Despite his carrying those doubts and guilts, Christina's tender reassurance made a difference. His load had eased by sharing his past with Christina. She had a way of making him think the future could be different. He started to believe that open wound might heal.

They stayed like that for a long time. Then slept.

Conor woke to Christina kissing his chest. Her hand brushed his chest hair lightly. He returned her kiss. Their lovemaking was silent and tender this time as if she wanted to heal his broken heart.

Conor woke with Christina still beside him. He watched the morning light slowly creep into the room. Soon, Christina's internal clock would have her up, ready to feed the horses. She would push him aside to care for them. He would soak up holding her while he could. Right now, the idea of letting go of her soft, placid body made him want to squeeze her tighter.

He sensed the moment she woke. She gave him a soft smile before her eyes widened and she rolled away from him. "It's daylight. I have to get moving. The horses will be stomping in their stalls."

"I think they can give me two minutes." He couldn't believe he thought they could discuss something as amazing as last night and cover it in two minutes.

"There's nothing to talk about. You're a grown man. I'm a grown woman. We had a nice night together. We didn't plan it. It happened. Let's leave it at that. I enjoyed it and I hope you did, too. We both know that can't happen again."

Her detached attitude made him think of the time a horse kicked him in the ribs. Painful with a lingering ache. She was pushing him away. It was nothing worse than what he'd planned to do to her. She just beat him to it. Maybe that was how it had to be.

Or did it? He shoved his guilt away. He brushed his palm over her bare nipple.

She moved his hand away. "Don't start that. I've got to get to the horses. I've got a full day ahead."

"Christina, I didn't see you coming."

"Sometimes we don't see what we should and just get caught up in it. Other times we don't want to see it. I've been there and done that. I can't,

I won't, do it again. It's too hard to come back from."

She climbed out of bed and started looking through clothes. Her room really was a mess. Just part of her charm.

"You sound like you're speaking from experience." Was she thinking of the jerk who had stolen from her, damaged her reputation and broken her heart? Conor wasn't him. Or was he?

"We agreed to no promises. Just for fun. We both needed it."

He hated her sounding so flippant and callous. Yet, he understood why she lashed out.

"What's the deal with the promises, Conor? I didn't ask for any."

Did he want to tell her? The words came out before he could stop them. "The deal is my father ran around on my mother and me." He hesitated. "I promised myself I would never do that to someone I cared about."

Her look turned perplexed. "Are you planning to go to another woman tonight?"

"No. I'm talking about being faithful to my wife."

Christina's face softened. "Conor, you were a good husband, and I have no doubt faithful, but she wouldn't want you to be alone. I believe we both need to take a step back."

"But I didn't mean…"

She raised a hand. "It's okay. I'm a big girl. I've disappointed people and they have disappointed me. I just make a point not to get too close." She pointed at him then her. "This is not any different. Let's not get too invested. Put it down to a moment of insanity."

Okay, that hurt. "You do know you spent the entire night with me. There were moments of insanity, but they were earth-shaking ones." Why was he tempted to argue with her? Wasn't she offering him what he wanted without him being the jerk who walked out on her after one night together? "Neither of us disappointed the other."

She blushed and looked away. "You know what I mean. It was good but that was yesterday, and this is now."

He climbed out of bed and took a step toward her. "You don't think it could be good here, right now and in broad daylight?"

Christina's eyes widened. A little puff of breath came from the O her mouth had formed. "That's not what I meant. I thought you wanted the same thing as I. That we had an agreement."

"We did but I refuse to have you diminish what we shared."

"That's not what I'm doing." With jerky steps she moved around the room, picking up clothes then letting them float to the floor once more.

"It sure sounded like that to me." He pulled on his pants, leaving them unzipped.

Her gaze traveled over his chest to the opening of his pants. "I didn't intend for it to."

"Good. I'm glad to hear that. It's a time I will remember with pleasure. I would like to think you will, too."

Her look met his. "Conor, you should have no fear of that. It was everything a woman dreams of. Thank you."

Her words bolstered him but now she made it sound like their time together was an experiment in a lab. No emotion. Maybe that was the point; there had been too much emotion on both their parts. He hadn't been prepared for the connection between them. Had it been the same for her? He needed time to analyze it, adjust to it and accept it. She could need that as well.

"Conor—"

"I've got to see about moving Gold today. It's time for him to start working out where he will be running." The last thing he needed was for her to tell him how wonderful, how perfect, it had been and how it would never happen again.

Her eyelids lowered then rose again. "I understand."

"Will you check on Gold while I start breakfast? It will be waiting."

Half an hour later Conor stepped out the back

door of the house and headed for the barn. Breakfast was getting cold. Christina had been gone long enough. Guilt had swept over him the second her sweet smell left the room. He had broken his vow to himself. His feelings roiled inside him. He couldn't sort them out, even if he wanted to. He shouldn't have taken Christina to bed even as pleasurable as it was. He had done her an injustice.

He wasn't staying in Kentucky. He wasn't any better than the guy who had hurt her. Conor wouldn't be around to support and care for her. He belonged at home in Ireland with his memories and his family.

She wouldn't leave Kentucky. Even if he dared to ask her. She was too firmly established here, in her horses, in her dream of starting a rehabilitation farm.

Bloody hell, he'd really made a mess of things.

To have acted on emotion instead of his brain was unforgivable at his age. He should know better. But her kisses, her body pressed to his…

His actions were so unlike him. He had always been practical, solid, thoughtful, yet Christina managed to make him throw out all his thinking abilities and go with feelings. The desire to live in the here and now became too strong.

Christina sat across the table from Conor. He silently sipped his second cup of coffee as if it was a normal morning instead of the one after an amazing night in her bed. She came close to groaning out loud. It had been she who had invited him in.

He'd come searching for her when she hadn't returned. She reluctantly agreed to the meal, but it had become a tense affair, making the food taste like hay.

Conor had been standing on the back stoop waiting, watching the barn when she had come out. She'd stayed longer than usual, needing to think. The moment she appeared he'd gone inside.

What had she expected? Hadn't she known the score before they made love? She was a grown woman. Hadn't they both agreed to no promises? Just the one night. Then why was she letting the idea that there might be more between them grow? She knew better.

Hadn't her past decisions proven that she didn't have what it took to last? She hadn't been good enough then and what made her think she was now? Could she ever keep a man like Conor?

He wasn't over his wife.

Somehow, her future didn't look as happy as it once had.

"Christina, stop it." Conor's bark jerked her out of her thoughts.

She looked at him over her mug. "What?"

"Thinking. I want us to remain friends," he came close to growling.

"We are friends."

His voice softened. "I certainly hope so." He sighed. "I'm going to Churchill Downs today. Gold will be moved there tomorrow. I have to make sure all is ready for him. He must pass inspection. I need to see if there is something more I need to do. Is there anything you need from there?"

Her chest tightened. She knew the day would come when Gold and Conor would leave. It had been inevitable. What she hadn't expected was for it to affect her so. Maybe it was a good thing. She could start getting used to him not being there. Conor might as well leave for good now. At least she could start getting used to the idea because in a little over a week he would return to Ireland.

"No. I have to go Monday for orientation anyway." By then she would have moved past this dreary mood over Conor. She needed to make a good impression, and showing up looking sad and lonely wasn't going to be the answer.

"I'll be moving into a hotel in Louisville close to the racetrack that Mr. Guinness has secured. I need to be closer than this to Gold. But I still plan to attend the party on Saturday night. Will you pick me up since you know the way?"

"I can do that." She looked into her coffee cup as if it had the answers to why her heart hurt.

"I'll be sure to let you know the information about where I'm staying."

The finality of it all saddened her more. But this was how she'd wanted it. He had agreed. It was for the best. She pushed back from the table, leaving half her breakfast on her plate. "Okay. That sounds like a plan. I need to get to work now."

That was what she should be worried about. Focused on. Her new business. She needed to make that her priority, and not worrying about Conor. Still, the thought of his kisses and caresses made her shiver. If she could force them into a box in her mind and close the top, she'd be better off. With some determination she'd get through the next week and then he would be gone.

She picked up her plate, cleaned it off and placed it in the sink. "Thanks for breakfast. I'll see you later."

Half an hour later she heard Conor's truck go down the drive. Her shoulders sagged. Why did she feel relieved and lonely at the same time? How had the man managed to matter so much in such a short time?

Conor drove toward Louisville and Churchill Downs thinking less about where he was going and more about Christina. What had happened between them last night hadn't been something

SUSAN CARLISLE

139

he had imagined or planned for when he came to America. That might be the case, but he couldn't say he hadn't enjoyed being with Christina or that he wouldn't like to repeat the pleasure.

He wanted to respect the distance she had requested while at the same time he wanted to shake her and tell her they could figure something out. Maybe the problem was she had been the one to beat him to placing the boundaries.

Until recently, he would have said he would never be interested in another woman. That had changed because of Christina. Still, he couldn't give her what she wanted. A family. He couldn't go there again. But surely they could find a compromise because she had done the impossible, made him care again.

With little more than a week before the Kentucky Derby, the racecourse was already buzzing with more activity than it had been on his last visit. In just a few days, he would be a part of that. He would miss the calm, slow life of Seven Miles Farm and Stables. And Christina.

His work would really step up when Gold arrived tomorrow. The next day the trainer, along with his grooms and barn hand, would be there. It was Conor's job as the lead man on the scene to see that Gold was safely moved and checked into a barn. Today he would have a look at Gold's stable, but first Conor needed to check in with the clinic. It was time Gold really exercised. He needed to run and flex his muscles. The horse needed to get on the Breeze schedule.

Entering the clinic, he found the place busy as well.

Dr. Dillard came around the corner. "Hello, Doctor O'Brian. I was wondering when you would be in. It's about time to move into the barn, isn't it?"

"The plan is to do that tomorrow. Well over the hundred-and-three-hour limit for the horse to be on the premises."

"Indeed. Tell me, how has it worked out being at Doctor Mobbs's place?"

"Great. Gold seems to be in fine shape, and it's a quiet place to settle in." Conor did really love Christina's farm. If he lived in America, it would be the type of place he would like to have.

"Good to hear. Good to hear. I was wondering about sending others if necessary."

"I can't think of a better place." Conor meant it.

"How did you make out personally? I know the farm is a little farther from here than you would have liked."

"I made out fine." Was the man fishing for more than general information? Too fine, in fact. He had started to feel like it was home. "She was kind enough to rent me a room when I realized there was a misunderstanding about how close I needed to be to Gold."

"Well, I'm glad it worked out. I'm a little surprised she agreed. Christina has had a difficult time during the last couple of years. I'm an acquaintance of her uncle, who is also a vet. I felt the need to help her where I could."

"I know she appreciates it. She is an excellent veterinarian. I believe you will be pleased to have her on your staff."

"I believe you are correct. That's why I suggested her place and have given her a position working here during the week. The man she got hooked up with dragged her name through the mud."

If Conor ever met that guy, he might do something he wouldn't be proud of.

"The program she is starting is worthwhile," Dr. Dillard continued, "I would like to see it flourish."

Conor would, too. "She has a wonderful place for it and she is excellent at that type of work."

"So I understand. Well, is there something I can do for you?"

Conor shook his head. "No, I just need to check in and see if there is anything required that I haven't already covered, then I'm on my way to check out the stall."

"I'll have someone call for a golf cart to take you to the barn. You'll need to plan to walk back."

"I can do that." He shook his hand.

The man nodded. "I'll see you Saturday evening, then."

Conor waited outside the clinic. Soon, a man in a golf cart pulled up. On the ride, he jostled along the gravel road between the barns and past the grassy area where horses were being washed and groomed. The man pulled to a sharp stop in front of a white barn with red flower baskets hanging from the porch. Gold would be installed in the second stall from the right. He got off the golf cart and the driver took off.

Conor strolled over to the barn stall, opened the door and entered. He checked the walls, the gate and feeding trough for any hanging wood, paint or any other material that could harm Gold. It all looked good and was spotlessly clean. Outside lay a strip of grass and a grooming area. Gold should do well here. Everything looked satisfactory.

He started his walk back to his truck. A golf cart came by and came to a sudden stop in front of him, throwing gravel.

The woman whom he had been introduced to as Christina's cousin looked at him. "Aren't you the guy that was with Christina the other day?"

"Yes. I'm Conor O'Brian. I'm staying at her place."

She looked around. "Is she here today?"

"No, I'm seeing about moving a horse I'm responsible for here tomorrow."

A look of disappointment came over her face. "Well, that's good. Do you need a ride somewhere?"

"As a matter of fact, I could use one back to my truck."

She patted the golf cart seat. "Then hop in."

Conor did and she took off like a shot. He grabbed the support bar holding the roof.

"Have you been enjoying your stay in America? At Christina's?" She glanced at him.

"Kentucky reminds me of Ireland. The grass, rolling hills and of course the horses."

"I have to admit I'm a little surprised Christina let you stay at her place."

Conor studied the woman for a moment. Was she trying to get at something? No, she was just making conversation. "Let's just say it wasn't her idea. She wasn't left much choice."

"She's remained closed off for the last few years, unfortunately. To everyone. Especially men."

"I understand she has good reason. I heard he was a real piece of work."

Callie studied him a second. "She told you about him?"

"Yeah, she told me about what happened."

"She must really like you. As far as I know outside of a handful of people, she's never told anyone about what really happened."

Conor couldn't help but find pleasure in that knowledge. Yet, he still held out about the baby.

"I could tell by the way she looked at you the other day she really liked you." Callie made a right turn that almost slung him off the cart.

Christina looked at him a certain way? For some reason that made his chest expand. "I'd say we have become friends over the last two weeks."

"She hasn't let anybody close enough to be a friend in years. You must be somebody special."

He had no idea if that was true.

"I'm glad she has the job on the veterinary team. I know she really wanted that."

Conor was glad Christina was getting something she really wanted, too. "Yes, she puts great stock in working here during Derby week."

"Understandably. She had a difficult time and people were not kind to her, even though she wasn't the one found guilty. That jerk she thought she was in love with didn't do her any favors." Venom filled Callie's voice.

"That's my truck right up there. The red one." He pointed ahead of them.

Callie pulled to a halt beside the truck and he climbed out.

"It was nice to see you again. I'm sure I'll be

seeing you around in the next week. Tell Christina I look forward to seeing her as well." Callie smiled.

"Thanks for the ride."

The visit to the track had been fruitful professionally but more so personally. It certainly had given him food for thought where Christina was concerned. If he'd been trying to push Christina into the background of his life today, he hadn't achieved that.

CHAPTER SEVEN

CHRISTINA WOKE AT the first ring of the phone and picked it up on the second. Truly, she hadn't been asleep. Her night had been spent thinking about Conor on the other side of the house.

She had known better and gotten what she deserved.

Conor was still hung up on his dead wife. He lived thousands of miles away. There was just no way a relationship between them would work. Apparently, he felt the same way. It didn't take him long to freeze her out.

He was a nice guy. But she'd believed Nelson had been, too. Her judgment of character had been way off. What made her think it wasn't the same with Conor? She couldn't afford to put her heart out there again and have it broken.

She ended the call. Scrambling out of bed she quickly dressed. She didn't get many midnight calls, but when she did, she knew it was an emergency. She never questioned whether she needed to go or not. People who owned high-strung horses recognized when there was a problem. Many thought they could handle things themselves so when they asked for her, she took it seriously. It wasn't something that would wait until morning.

She was in the kitchen pulling on her boots when Conor walked in wearing only sports shorts. He pushed his fingers through his hair making it stand up in places. He appeared rumpled and sexy. She looked away and pushed those thoughts from her mind. Now wasn't the time anyway. Later wouldn't be, either. Or she wouldn't let it be.

"What's going on?" His voice was low and gravelly with sleep.

"I have an emergency. I'm sorry. I didn't mean to wake you."

"In the barn?" His eyes turned anxious.

"No, it's one of my clients." She shoved her foot into the other boot.

"You're going off this time of the night by yourself?" He sounded genuinely concerned.

Maybe he did care more than he wanted to admit. "I've done it plenty of times."

"I'm going with you."

A little thrill of heat filled her chest, but she pushed it down. "That's not necessary."

"I'll be ready to go by the time you are." He headed to his room without giving her a chance to argue.

As good as his word, Conor arrived at her truck just as she was ready to go. She climbed behind the steering wheel. "You don't have to do this."

"Sure, I do."

She took off down the lane. They remained silent as she drove through the night.

Finally, he asked, "Where are we going?"

"The Owens' Farm. He has a horse down. He said she has been off her feed. He went to check on her before going to bed and found her on the floor." Christina gave the truck more gas.

"That's all the information you have?"

She glanced at him in the dim light. Even in it she could make out the handsome cut of his jaw. "I know my clients well enough to know when they call it's something I need to react to."

"Okay, that's reasonable. How far is this farm?"

"We're almost there." She made a left turn into the gravel drive.

When Christina pulled up near the barn, Mr. Owen stood under the night-light with his hands in his pockets. He walked toward them. She climbed out and grabbed her bag from the side storage compartment of the truck. Conor joined them with his bag in hand.

"How's she doing?" Christina asked, falling in step with the older man on his way into the barn.

"Like I said, I came out to check on the horses before I went to bed. I found Joy laying on the floor of the stall. She had been kicking something awful. That's when I called you."

"Have you changed her food?"

"No, but I noticed she was off her feed yesterday and circling the stall more than usual. I thought I'd watch her another day, then this. I should have called you earlier."

The poor man looked so distraught she placed her hand on his arm. "We're here to help. We'll do all we can to make it better." She looked back at Conor. "This is Doctor O'Brian. Together we'll figure it out."

She never thought of it that way before, but they did make a good team. They played off each other's skills and experiences well. She enjoyed working with Conor. That was something she couldn't have said about Nelson.

They entered the barn, Mr. Owen directing them down the main hall to a stall on the other end. The horse was still on the floor. Groaning and twitching and kicking her feet.

"Mr. Owen, I need you to hold her head and speak softly to her."

When the farmer had control of the horse, Christina went to her knees beside the animal and placed her hand on the horse's belly. It was distended and hard. Conor came down beside her. He gave the horse the same examination.

"Will you do the general vitals while I listen for stomach sounds?"

Conor rose and picked up his bag. "I'll take care of it."

Thankfully, the horse had chosen to settle in the middle of the stall, giving them working room in the small area. Christina pulled her stethoscope from her bag. After placing the ends in her ears, Christina positioned the bell on the horse's abdomen to listen. The bowel sounds were just as she suspected. The horse had a bowel obstruction.

She put her stethoscope back and then started running her hand along the belly of the horse. "Mr. Owen, this became bad between when and when?"

"I was out here at eight. I came back about midnight. Just before I called you."

She looked out the stall door. "None of your other horses are having any problems?"

The man shook his head. "None that I can see."

Conor's look met hers. "Her face is swollen, and there is bruising around the eyes."

Were they thinking the same thing? As if Conor had read her mind, he nodded.

She took a deep breath. "Mr. Owen, I believe Joy has a large colon volvulus. You may have heard it called a 'twisted gut.' If we don't do surgery right away the intestines may burst. Joy will die if that happens."

Concern tightened the man's face. "I understand. So when is this surgery?"

"As soon as we can get ready."

The man's brows rose. "You'll be doing it here?"

She nodded. "Yes, we have no time to get Joy to a clinic."

The man's eyes widened.

"I need you to get me a large sheet that you don't want returned. It will have to go in the trash. Also hot water and soap. I need you to do so quickly."

Mr. Owen patted the horse's neck. "I'll go to the house right now."

"I'll get the supplies out of the truck." Conor moved toward the stall door. "You have this, Christina."

"Thanks. It's been a while since I've had to do serious surgery."

He gave her a tight smile. "I'll be here with you." Then he walked out of the barn.

It was nice to have another competent veterinarian there with her. In an odd way, Conor made a nice security blanket. She had learned to trust him, at least when it came to their work.

While he was gone she had brushed the hay away from the horse's belly using her boot. After that, she prepared a sedative so the horse would be calm and pain-free while they worked.

Conor returned with handfuls of supplies in a basket she kept in the storage area for such an occasion. "Check and see if I brought everything you need. I'll stay here with the horse."

Christina reviewed everything and found it well prepared. "Conor, talk this through with me. We are going to need to scab the incision site with soap and hot water."

Conor nodded. "The incision will have to be long. This surgery always requires a few more inches than expected just because you need to see so much of the area to find the problem."

At least her and Conor's discussion was calming Christina's nerves. "I need to give a bolus dose of antibiotics before we start."

"Agreed." Conor handed her what she needed.

She drew an amount up in a syringe. "Check me on this. I don't want to have any questions asked."

Conor studied the syringe a moment. "Yes, it looks correct to me."

She then went to the horse and gave her a shot in the hip.

Mr. Owen returned. "Here are two sheets. And the bucket has the water in it." He sat it on the floor and handed her the sheets.

Christina placed one over the wall in reserve. She laid one on the ground at the horse's belly and tucked in under her. Conor set out the supplies nearby. She was thankful for his help.

"Mr. Owen, I'm gonna need you to hold her head." The middle-aged man went down on his knees beside the horse.

She gave Conor a perplexed look when he left. He soon returned with a stool and placed it beside Mr. Owen. Conor was a good guy.

She pulled on plastic gloves then drew up a sedative and administered it to the horse. Soon, the horse had relaxed.

"Conor, will you prepare the incision area?"

He, too, pulled on gloves. He washed the area with soap and water. He then opened a surgical kit and removed the razor. After shaving the surgical area, he scrubbed it with antiseptic.

Conor moved to the side, and she took the space. He handed her the scalpel, and she made the incision.

"Should I go larger?"

"Another two inches. We need to be sure we can see everything." He watched beside her.

Christina did as he suggested. With the horse's abdomen open they went in search of the obstruction. She removed a handful of intestines. "Do you see it?"

"There it is," Conor said. "Down on the left."

She shifted the intestines so she could see. He was right. There was the twisted cord. "Let's get this resected and repaired."

Conor said, "Can you resect it while I hold it?

Clip off on both ends at the same time. We don't need it to build up and burst."

She did as he requested. With that done, she took the scissors from her surgical kit and cut one end below the twist and then the other, and removed the piece of intestine.

"Excellent work."

Conor's praise washed through her. He handed her the needle and thread. She quickly stitched the two remaining ends together.

"I don't know that I've seen nicer stitches."

She smiled.

Working together, they slowly and gently returned the intestines to their place.

"Now, to get her closed up. You stitch and I'll pull the skin together." Conor handed her the needle and thread.

Together they worked until the incision had been sutured.

"While I clean up, why don't you check vitals?" Christina suggested.

"That, I can do." He washed in the bucket and started on the vitals.

By the time she'd cleaned up and he'd finished, the horse was waking.

"Mr. Owen, how are you doing?" Conor placed a hand on the man's shoulder.

"I'm well, and very impressed. You two working together is a show."

"A good one, I hope." Conor grinned.

"Certainly."

Christina had to agree. She and Conor did work well together along with doing other things well. "Thank you. We now need to get Joy on her feet. She needs to be led around for a while. Large animals don't need to lie on the floor. We need to work the anesthesia out of her system and get her organs active. Mr. Owen, you pull on her lead while Conor and I nudge her from behind."

The older man rose stiffly from the stool. She and Conor positioned themselves at the horse's back and pushed.

After a few minutes of encouragement, the horse wobbled to her feet and stood.

"Good job. Now, Mr. Owen, please lead her around in a circle. We need to get her loosened up."

She and Conor backed out of the stall.

The horse staggered but soon found steady footing.

Conor leaned against her. "Nice job, Doctor."

She grinned. "You, too. You know we're going to need to stay here and watch over Joy for a couple of hours."

"I do."

She studied the horse. "I'm sorry I can't send

you home because I might need something off the truck."

"I wouldn't leave anyway." He sounded like he meant it.

She looked at him and smiled. "I guess you wouldn't."

Conor leaned against the stall wall. "We should encourage Mr. Owen to go to bed. He looks dead on his feet."

"I agree." How like Conor to show concern for another. The man got to her.

She entered the stall and took the lead from the man. "Why don't you get some rest? Conor and I have to be here anyway. We can take care of her from here. You may need to give her some attention after we're gone. So go."

Mr. Owen gave her a weak smile. "Thank you. I think I'll take you up on that."

She started walking the horse around the stall. Conor walked out with Mr. Owen but soon returned with a blanket and a couple of folding chairs.

"Go have a seat and let me have a turn." His hand brushed hers as he took the lead.

Her unruly heart jumped at the touch. She had been glad to have his knowledge and help. He had become a fixture in her life. It hurt to think about him leaving. Despite her better judgment, she would miss him.

* * *

Conor grinned. Christina had piled hay in the hallway then laid the blanket over it before curling up on it. Now she slept. This was becoming a weekly event for them to spend one night in a barn. Funny thing was he could not think of anywhere he would rather be except in Christina's bed.

He felt honored she trusted him to watch over the horse. When he had first arrived, she had mistrusted him at every turn. Slowly, her attitude had changed. He found it rewarding. His feelings for her weren't doing him any favors, or her, either. He wouldn't offer her what she wanted. He couldn't go there again. He couldn't take that chance again.

Yet, he smiled down at Christina. They were different, lived in different parts of the world and their lives were damaged. The negatives were too many.

She would be appalled to know that in her sleep she looked angelic. That her tough exterior had slipped and turned vulnerable.

He sat a chair near where she lay and leaned back against the wall of a stall. From there he could clearly see the horse tied in its stall. The animal would not feel like being frisky for some time. He set the timer on his watch to go off in an hour. He would walk the horse a couple of turns, letting Christina rest as long as possible. He would also do the driving home.

He continued to keep watch over her and the horse until light peeked under the doors of the barn. He shook Christina awake.

She opened her eyes and made a long catlike stretch. Which might have been the sexiest thing he'd ever seen.

"I didn't mean to sleep so long. You were supposed to wake me."

He shrugged. "You looked too peaceful."

Her attention went to the stall. "How's Joy doing?"

Conor liked that she had no doubt he would have taken care of the horse while she slept. "I've been walking her every hour. In fact, it's time for a walk now."

"I'll do it."

He watched carefully to see if the horse faltered or showed pain.

Christina smiled. "You know I could've done this without you but I'm glad I didn't have to."

He grinned. "That was a nice thing for you to say. I like knowing I'm needed. It has been too long."

She tied Joy up again. Picking up the blanket, she folded it then hung it over the back of the chair he had used.

"I'm surprised Mr. Owen hasn't been out

yet." She started down the barn hall and in came the man.

"Good morning. How is Joy doing?" He looked toward the horse with concern.

"Great. Conor and I are headed home. You call me if you need me. I'll be back to check on her tomorrow. I'll be gone next week working the Derby but if you need anything you call me and I'll see that you get help."

"That's a big deal to get to work the Derby. I understand only a handful are picked."

"She got it because she is one of the best." Conor's voice held pride.

Christina looked at him and softly smiled, her eyes bright.

"My wife and I don't miss a Derby Day. We look forward to it every year."

"My family wasn't any different," Christina said. "It's an honor to be included as part of the staff."

"It's past due for you. You were mistreated a couple of years ago."

Christina looked down. "Thank you for that. I'm glad to have this opportunity but working ten to twelve hours a day will be tough. Few people realize how much goes on behind the scenes."

"I know they'll be glad to have you." Mr. Owen lifted a bag. "My wife has fixed breakfast for you. Egg sandwiches and a thermos of coffee. You can bring the thermos back when you come again. She said to tell you she would've invited you in but thought you might like to get home to your beds."

Christina took the bag. "Please give her our thanks."

Conor's stomach growled. "Mine in particular."

Christina said, "We'll give Joy one more look then we'll go. It's been a day. I need to get home and check on the horses."

She and Conor did their final analysis and headed for the truck, leaving Mr. Owen with instructions on how to continue Joy's care.

"I appreciate you helping out."

"Glad I was here to help. You were really good in there." He nodded toward the barn. "Impressive, in fact."

"Thanks. That's nice to hear."

Conor studied her a moment. "You haven't been told that before?"

"I didn't get much positive reinforcement from my mother growing up."

"You should be given it often." He meant it. Christina was an amazing veterinarian and equally amazing woman.

"I really appreciate it when I hear it." Christina placed supplies into the side storage bin of the truck. She yawned.

"You're tired. I'll drive home."

On the way to her house, she leaned back

against the headrest and closed her eyes. When her head bobbed, he guided it down until it rested on his thigh. She sighed as she settled in.

Disappointment filled him when he turned into the drive. He would have to give up having her close.

Christina woke to warm, hard muscle beneath her cheek. She'd fallen asleep on Conor. She'd kept a number of long days but staying up all night wasn't her norm. With the Derby week ahead, she needed her rest.

It had been so nice to have Conor along tonight for the help and even the reassurance. She didn't do emergency operations very often and it was nice to have assistance, especially professional assistance. It had also been helpful to have somebody who took turns seeing about the horse.

She felt confident Joy would recover well. It might be touch and go for a few days, but overall, she would be fine.

When they reached her farm she hopped out of the truck. "I'm gonna go check on the horses. You're welcome to the shower first."

"I'm coming to help you." His firm tone stopped any argument. "I'll check on Gold as well. We're both exhausted and we can both go out there and get everything done in half the time."

In short order they finished caring for the horses and feeding them.

On the way to the house Conor kept pace with her. "Gold will be moving this afternoon. Thank goodness my plans were for later in the day. There is such an influx of horses at the Downs, so this afternoon appointment was the earliest I could get."

Sadness washed over Christina. She would miss the horse. More than that, she would miss Conor. She stepped on the stoop and turned to look down at Conor. "Thank you again for your help last night. I especially appreciate you staying up all night after I fell asleep on you."

"Not a problem. I was glad I was here to help."

She gave him a tight smile when she really wanted to kiss him. "I still appreciate it."

"I was glad I could be here for you."

"You're a really nice guy, Conor, and an excellent veterinarian."

"Thank you for the compliment. I'm not sure I wouldn't like the adjectives to be reversed."

"You are an excellent guy and a nice vet." Christina couldn't help herself. Her lips brushed his.

Conor's hands found her waist. "I think you can do better than that. In fact, I know you can." His mouth sealed hers before he pulled her against him, pressing her tightly against his hard body.

The kiss deepened. Their tongues tangled, searching and giving pleasure.

This is what she'd been wanting and missing since she had given her speech the day before. The one filled with lics. It would still be worth it to have him near, even if it hurt when he left. She would take advantage of what time they had for as long as he would let her.

Christina wrapped her arms around his neck and held tightly. She joined him in the kiss. The heat of desire spread through her. This man was honest and good. She could trust him. It has been too long since she had been able to say that. He'd proven himself.

Conor pulled away. "I'm sorry. I couldn't help myself."

"I'm not sorry at all."

He kissed her again. His need strong between them. "You know if we share a shower we could find a little more time to sleep."

She giggled. "I suspect that we would use it up in another way."

He gave her a deep, wet, suggestive kiss. "I suspect you're right. Let's go inside. I need to touch you."

His hand held hers as she opened the door. In the kitchen they kicked off their boots as if they had done the actions together their entire lives. Finished, she smiled at him. He returned it.

She took his hand again and led him down the hall into the bath. Inside, she turned on the water. Her fingers went to the buttons of his shirt. Slowly, she opened them.

He pulled his shirt from his pants. She pushed it over his shoulders. It dropped to the floor. He chuckled. "I'm not sure this is a time-saving operation. But I do know if I don't take all the chances I'm given to be in your arms, I'll regret it. Forever."

Her hands went to his belt and worked it open. She treasured the intake of his breath when her fingers brushed his skin. Slowly, she unzipped his pants and maneuvered them over his extended manhood. With her hands at his waist she pushed his jeans to the floor.

He stepped out of them.

Her hands went to his underwear, but he stopped her. "My turn to undress you."

Gently, he pulled her T-shirt over her head. With it removed, he kissed the top of one breast then the other while he reached around her and daftly unhooked her bra. He pulled it away and dropped it into the pile of clothing on the floor. His hands made short work of removing her pants. "Honey, we will not make it to the bed."

She relished the deep, throaty sound of his accent as he nuzzled her ear.

"Mmm, that's okay with me."

CHAPTER EIGHT

CHRISTINA STRETCHED HER arm out across the bed. Her hand came in contact with a hard, warm body. A stream of pleasure flowed through her. Conor was there beside her.

She smiled, enjoying him and the sunshine flooding through the window. She could get used to this—waking up next to Conor.

She rolled enough in his direction to sneak a peek to see if he was awake. A blue gaze met hers.

"Good morning. Or should I say afternoon?" He grinned at her.

"It's not afternoon yet but almost. Have you been awake long?"

His hand brushed her breast. "I was just waiting on you to open your eyes."

A tingle flowed through her. "You were?"

Conor's hand moved to the curve of her hip as his eyes narrowed. "I was."

She rolled closer to him. "Is there something I can do for you?"

"Most definitely."

"Did you have something particular in mind?" She ran her hand over his bare chest.

"I do." His lips found hers.

She rose over him to straddle his hips. "Aren't you expecting a truck and trailer for Gold soon? Maybe this should wait," she teased.

His hands caressed the skin of her sides. "No, it can't."

"I should get to work." She moved to climb off him.

Conor held her in place, sliding her over him, filling her. "I don't think so. We both need to take time to enjoy what we have."

He left off *while it lasts*. But she was well aware of it. For a change, she would do just that. Her lips brushed his as she lifted her hips until he almost lost her and she plunged down again.

Conor made a sexy sound of pleasure in his throat.

She said, "I don't disagree."

Later, as they pulled on their boots, Conor asked, "Can we talk a minute?"

The last time that had happened she had said some stupid things, and she didn't want that to happen again. "I thought we had been. In more ways than one."

That brought a wolfish grin to Conor's lips that soon slipped to a wry tightness of his mouth. "I have to move into town. I can't be this far from

Gold and the racetrack. With the security in the backside during the week before the Derby, I'm needed nearby."

"I get it."

He stepped closer. "I have a room at a hotel. Maybe you could spend the week with me there since you must be in town all week. It would make for a longer day to have to drive back and forth."

"I have the horses to see about." Even if she wanted to go, she had responsibilities and a business to consider.

"Can't you get someone to see about them?"

She leaned her head to the side in thought. "Maybe I could for a few days but not the entire time."

"At least say you will find someone for Sunday morning." Conor sounded close to begging. "That way you can stay with me after the party."

"I guess I could do that."

"I wish you would." He gave her sad eyes.

"I'll see what I can do between now and Saturday evening to get some help." She was already thinking of people she could call.

At 2:00 p.m. the truck and trailer to transport Gold rolled up her drive. Conor waited at the barn to meet it. Not soon after the truck stopped Conor led Gold into the trailer. Earlier, he'd collected all of the horse's supplies and placed them in his truck.

They both had examined Gold carefully to make sure he was well and fit. He would not be allowed on the backside unless he could pass the rigid Kentucky Horse Racing Commission list of protocols. Conor reviewed all his paperwork for shots dates and blood tests and how they were handled. All that information must be in order before Gold would be allowed on the property. After the horse was in a stall on Churchill Downs property, he would have limited access to Gold and only when security was around.

With Gold secure in the trailer, Christina joined Conor beside his truck. "I'll see you Saturday evening. Since I know the area better, why don't I pick you up at your hotel?"

"No. Once again, you are my date and I would like to see about getting us there. Please just plan to meet me in the lobby of the hotel at six. I've got it from there."

She started to open her mouth.

He gave her a direct look. "Christina, please do not argue with me."

"Okay."

Conor gave her a quick kiss on the lips as the truck and trailer started down the drive. "I have to go. I will see you Saturday evening. I'll call if I have a chance." He hopped in his truck and rolled down the window. "I will miss you."

She smiled, giving him a wave. A heavy cloak of sadness settled over her shoulders. This was just a taste of the feelings she would have when he returned to Ireland but on a larger scale. Then he would truly be gone.

She had brought this on herself. She'd have to live with that knowledge, but at least she will have had him for a while.

Saturday evening Conor paced back and forth in the lobby of the hotel in downtown Louisville, watching for Christina. He had expected her five minutes ago. Normally prompt, it was not like her to arrive late. Had she decided not to attend? No, she wouldn't do that. She had been working toward this opportunity to become a part of the veterinarian group at the Derby for too long. He pulled out his cell phone and looked at it. There was no text from her.

She must be nervous about being in a group of veterinarians who had judged her just a few years earlier. She worried too much about the past. She had proved herself not guilty and also qualified to care for racehorses.

With a release of fear, he saw her enter through the automatic sliding glass doors. She was a vision of loveliness, and she had no idea. Wearing a simple dark green dress, she appeared confident and dependable. She looked perfect to impress.

Little earrings dangled from her earlobes. The bit of shimmer had him wanting to bite at the sweet spot behind her ears. He had never expected to feel like this about a woman again. Especially for one who did not want him to. Going from not feeling anything for a woman to this intense need made his middle uneasy. Worse, he did not know what to do about it.

The more time they spent together, the greater the difficultly he would have in giving her up, yet he could not stay away from Christina. He kept reminding himself that this situation was temporary. After he left, he wouldn't be able to forget her. The past two nights alone had proved him wrong. He had been miserable without her. He'd quickly learned he would be willing to take any time she would give him.

Christina stopped when she saw him. A smile formed on her lips that had little to do with finding him and everything to do with her being aware of him as a man. His blood heated and his chest swelled. That sparkle in her eyes he would treasure for the rest of his life. She looked him over from head to toe.

Then she stepped up to him. Into his personal

space. "You look very handsome." She ran her
hand under one of the lapels of his suit.

He suddenly had no desire to attend a party but
to have one just for them in his room. "Thank you.
You look lovely, Christina."

"I love the way you say my name. Your accent is super sexy, making it more special." She
gave him a quick kiss on the lips. He reached for
her, but she stepped back before he could take
her in his arms. Apparently, she was more aware
of where they were than he. "We better go or
we're going to be later than we should be. I had
to change a couple of times."

"Was that because of me or the people at the
party?"

"Both. Did I tell you how glad I am to have you
going with me?"

"No, but I am glad to hear it. When Doctor Dillard mentioned it the first time, I wasn't sure you
thought it was a good idea." He grinned.

"Okay, maybe I've changed my mind about you
some."

He pulled her close for a moment and kissed
her temple. "I'm glad to hear it. You know you
really shouldn't worry. You are the most amazing
person I know, inside and out."

"Do you say nice things to all the girls you go
to a party with?"

He gave her waist a gentle squeeze. "Only to you. After all, I haven't been to a party in years."

"Well, I am honored to be with you tonight." She kissed him on the cheek.

He nudged her toward the door. "We have admired each other enough tonight to create cavities in our teeth with the sugar. We should go."

She grinned. "I was rather enjoying it."

"We can try it again later."

Outside the lobby door, Conor waved his hand and a car pulled up.

Christina looked from him to the car and back again. "What's going on here?"

"I rented a driver for the night."

"That wasn't necessary. You shouldn't have spent all that money."

Conor waved the driver back to his seat and opened the car door for her. "You let me worry about that. I wanted to sit back here with you and enjoy the ride."

They settled into the backseat. She provided the driver with the address as they moved into traffic.

Conor took her hand in his. "I missed you. It's been too long. How are things? The horses?"

"I saw a couple of clients and spent the rest of the time in the barn."

"Did you find somebody to care for the horses tomorrow?" He brushed the pad of his thumb over the back of her hand.

"I made a few calls and found somebody I can trust. He's done it for one night before but he's willing to do it for three or four."

He leaned his forehead against hers. "So you will stay with me tonight?"

She gave him a shy smile. "If you still want me to?"

Conor pulled her hip against him. "Never question that I want you."

The driver pulled the car into the curved drive of a large redbrick two-story home with white columns and a wide porch across the front. The lights were shining in all the windows.

When the driver stopped at the front door, Conor climbed out and offered his hand. She took it. With a gentle squeeze he released it, closed the car door and offered his arm. Christina took it, holding tighter than necessary.

She was nervous about facing her colleagues. He was glad he would be there for her. She must have lived through an emotional ordeal for it to linger this long. But hadn't his wife's death done the same to him?

They entered the house and were directed along an elegant hallway to the open French doors at the back of the house. It looked out into a wide-open yard with a few aged trees. Among them hung white paper lanterns that lit the area along with lights from the house. To one side were four long tables laden with food, and also a man turning beef on a spit in the ground. Other round tables were spread out around the yard set for dining.

"Wow, this is beautiful," Christina said beside him.

"It does look nice, but the smell of meat cooking has my attention."

She smiled. "Always the cook."

"Hey, you haven't been complaining."

She hadn't. In fact, she hated returning to packaged food. "The only thing I can complain about is that I've gained almost ten pounds."

He leaned close. "And every one looks good on you."

"There you are, Christina. Good you could come." Dr. Dillard walked toward them. "And Doctor O'Brian. Nice to see you again."

Conor offered his hand. "Please call me Conor. Thanks for having us tonight."

Dr. Dillard shook it. "You're welcome. I understand you got your horse into the Downs stable without any trouble the other day."

"Yes, with a few hours to spare from those required." Conor took Christina's hand.

His attention went to the action for a moment before his look returned to Conor's. Dr. Dillard smiled. "We do have our rules for a reason."

"Understood. We have ours in Ireland as well."

Dr. Dillard glanced toward a woman waving at him. "My wife is calling. I must greet other guests. Please make yourselves at home. I'll bring my wife around to meet you soon." With that, he strolled off.

They moved to the drinks table and picked one then went to stand under a tree.

"Do you know anyone here?" Conor asked.

"I recognize a few people but most of them I have no idea who they are. People who work the race come from all over the state. It's an honor to do so."

Soon, Dr. Dillard asked for the group's attention. He gave a short welcome and stated that the party would be the fun before the busy week ahead.

That drew a ripple of laugher from everyone. Conor wasn't sure about what that meant but he was confident he would soon learn. By then some of Christina's anxiety had mellowed. For that he was grateful, but he remained close to her anyway.

Dr. Dillard introduced his wife to everyone, and she gave them directions on how to go about getting their food and encouraged them to sit wherever they wished.

Conor and Christina lined up on one side of the long tables. Picking up their plates, they moved through the buffet line. It was some of the most delicious-looking food he had seen since arriving in Kentucky.

"I hope you like barbecue," Christina said over her shoulder.

"I love it."

With full plates, they found an empty table. They settled into their chairs and started to eat. Other couples joined them until there were only two places left. These were soon taken by two men. As each new person joined them, everyone went around the table introducing themselves. Once again, they circled the table with names.

After Christina introduced herself, one of the men gave her an odd look. "Aren't you the veterinarian who was caught selling your drugs a few years back? I'm surprised you were invited to work at the racecourse."

Conor felt and saw Christina stiffen. This could only be her worst nightmare.

"Yes, I'm she, but I was not guilty." Her fork made no noise when she placed it on her plate.

The man poked his companion with his elbow. "Don't you remember that case?"

The other man grunted and continued to eat.

The first man returned to the conversation. "Still, I'm surprised they considered you for this group."

"I assure you I've been officially vetted. And can do the job."

Conor had heard enough. Christina didn't have to sit here and listen to this and neither did he. "I believe you owe Doctor Mobbs an apology."

The man took another swig of the amber liquor in his glass. He huffed. "For speaking the truth?"

Conor stood. "For being rude at the dinner table."

Christina put her hand on his arm. "It's not worth it."

"No, it's not," the man said it. "Especially since I'm speaking the truth."

Christina looked around the table. "If you'll excuse me, it was nice to meet you all."

Conor had to admit Christina held her head elegantly high as she rose, but he knew the willpower it took for her to do so. Inside, she would be a mass of raw emotions. She walked away with her shoulders squared.

He glared at the bad-mannered man. "I know I'm from another country, but I can recognize a drunk ass when I see one. You may not think so but you owe her an apology."

Conor caught up with Christina halfway down a path leading to a large barn in the fenced field behind the house. When he joined her he didn't say anything, he just fell into step beside her. Despite wanting to take her in his arms to comfort her, he resisted.

They continued walking. They were almost to

the barn before she spoke. "I'm never going to live down what happened."

"From what I understand, you don't have anything to live down."

"But it keeps cropping up. My home is here. I don't want to leave. It wasn't even me yet I'm the one that carries the stigma."

"It's not fair. I agree with that. But sometimes life is not fair."

She gave him a troubled look. "I'm sorry. You know that better than I."

"We're not talking about me tonight. We're talking about you. I was proud of you back there. You held your head high and you didn't let it show how much it hurt. And you didn't let me get into a fight. By the way, I'm not sure I could've whipped him."

Christina gave him a weak grin. "You know I do appreciate you defending me."

"It's not hard to defend you because you know what you're doing."

They continued walking, entering the open doors of the barn.

Conor had learned early in his relationship with Christina that being in a barn was where she thrived. She renewed her energy. The barn was where she went when she needed to think. Christina didn't hesitate to enter. They were overdressed for the place but she continued walking and he didn't stop her.

A couple of horses' heads hung over their stall gates. Christina patted the first horse's nose.

The sound of an animal in pain came from the back corner.

Christina hurried down the hall with Conor right behind her. They found a horse lying on its side.

She didn't hesitate to go down to her knees in her dress beside the horse and give it a quick examination with her hands. "This horse is in labor and it's coming breech. We need to get this colt out immediately, or the mare may die."

Conor said nothing.

She looked at Conor. He had gone still as a post. His skin had turn ghostly. A haunted look filled his eyes. He appeared terrified. "Conor? I'm going to need help."

"I'll go get Doctor Dillard."

"There's no time. You'll have to help me. I'm gonna need your muscles if we're gonna get this colt into the world safely."

"I…uh…"

"Conor! Go to the tack room and see what you can find that we might need."

Conor blinked and seemed to rejoin her from wherever he had gone. He hurried away.

While he was gone, she placed her ear to the

horse's bulging belly and listened to her steady heartbeat, hating that her stethoscope was in her bag at home.

Conor returned with an armful of supplies that included blankets and a bucket. His skin had turned to a more natural color, but his lips remained a thin, tight line.

"I saw a water faucet just outside the doors. I'll get some." Taking the bucket, he hurried off.

When he returned to the stall, he sat the bucket in the corner.

She rose and scrubbed her hands. Conor continued to stand there looking at the horse.

"We have to see if we can turn it."

"There are already two legs showing." Conor's words were monotone.

"Still, we have to try. I need your help." Christina didn't know what was going on with him, but what she did know was she couldn't do this without him. He had to focus on what was happening. Whatever problem he had he could deal with it afterward. Right now, she needed his help. "Have you done this before?"

He nodded. "A couple of times."

"Then that's twice as many as I have. I'm going to see if I can turn the colt." She laid a blanket on the hay behind the horse before going down on her knees. She worked to move the colt but made no real progress.

The horse moaned.

"My arm isn't long enough to reach the head." She looked at Conor. His eyes met hers. She watched his stricken look turn to one of determination.

He removed his jacket and hung it over the stall wall, rolling up his sleeves as far as he could then washed his hands and arms before he said, "Let me try."

He helped her stand then he lay down on his stomach. "Watch for the contractions and let me know when one is coming. I don't want my blood cut off."

With relief, Christina placed her hand on the horse's belly and felt. Conor was back with her. "I'll try to give you as much notice as I can."

"If I can use those moments between contractions, I'll have more room. Timing is everything."

"I'll do my best."

Conor met her gaze. "I never doubted it."

Seconds later she said, "Here comes one."

He removed his arm. When the contraction eased he went after the head of the colt. "I need to find the nose. I'm going to shift the head so it's not hung. The colt is still alive. I can feel its heart beating."

"Contraction coming," Christina announced.

Conor removed his arm. "It's still breech, but I believe we can pull this colt out now. During the next contraction, you'll need to pull while I work the head." He put his arm inside again. They waited, anticipation hanging in the air. "Ready? Let's go on my call. You need to make this a steady pull but as quickly as you can."

She looked at him. "I'll be ready. Contraction coming."

"Now," Conor said.

Christina pulled the legs. Conor's face contorted while he worked through the contraction. She could see the behind of the colt.

"Gentle tug. The head is in the right place," Conor encouraged.

Christina continued the pressure. Soon, the colt slipped from the mother. She and Conor were both breathing heavily when they finished. They didn't take a moment to catch their breaths before they were on their knees beside the colt. Christina quickly grabbed a blanket and began working it over the small animal, cleaning its mouth and face.

Conor, more himself than he had been, still looked worried but he joined her in rubbing.

"He's not breathing. We need to get some air in him."

Conor went to work across the colt's middle section using circles.

Christina was busy continuing to clean the baby's mouth and nostrils. She placed her mouth close to the animal's nose and breathed out. After a couple of times, the colt snorted and its eyes opened.

She looked at Conor. Pure relief showed on his face. Far more than she would have anticipated.

"I'll get Doctor Dillard." He went to the bucket and cleaned up then left the stall.

She sat back against the stable wall to catch her breath and watched him go. What was the matter with him? She'd had to force him to help her, which wasn't like him. He'd jumped in when needed when they had worked together before but tonight…

The mare worked her way to her feet before the new colt wobbled its way to her side. The mother licked it in acceptance. It was amazing to see new life come into the world. Would she ever get to have that moment? Conor's face popped into her mind. What would it be like to have his child?

Dr. Dillard rushed up. "O'Brian said you've been busy out here. She wasn't due for another week."

Christina didn't even have the energy to stand. He had to help her.

"I'm glad you two were here." Dr. Dillard fussed over her.

She looked around and didn't see Conor amongst the growing crowd. "It was pretty exciting, but all looks well now."

"I understand the colt was breech. I'm glad you both were here. I really appreciate it. This is my favorite horse. I have high hopes for this colt."

She went to the water bucket. "I'm glad we were, too."

"I heard about what happened at the dinner table. My apologies, Christina. That shouldn't have happened. He's been reprimanded. I put together a team and I expect everyone to work together. Saying stuff like that even when you're drunk isn't acceptable. You have more than proved your worth tonight."

"Thank you. And thank you for including me on the team and for your support."

Dr. Dillard's focus remained on the colt. "I'll see you at daylight Monday morning."

"I'll be there, sir." The crowd opened for her to walk through.

Christina moved away and headed for the house, searching out a bathroom and Conor. She looked everywhere and found him on the front porch. He stood with a shoulder against one of the columns, looking out at the night. What was going on? What had spooked him?

Shame filled Conor at his recent actions. He had failed Christina, his profession and himself. All of his feelings were tangled up in the loss of his baby. He could not think of anything else as he had watched the mare in labor. The horror of knowing his wife had killed herself when she'd been carrying his baby.

"Conor?"

The trepidation in Christina's voice only made him feel worse.

"Is everything all right?"

"I'm fine. Are you ready to go? If not, I'll call a taxi and leave the driver for you."

She went to him and wrapped her hand around his arm. "I'm not going anywhere without you. I'm ready to leave anyway. I'm a mess."

Soon, they were settled in the backseat of the car.

Christina held his hand while leaning her head against his shoulder, yet she said nothing. The driver maneuvered through the traffic. Before long, they were back at the hotel.

After the way he had acted, he dreaded asking when they reached the lobby, "Do you still want to come up? I'll understand if you don't."

She looked unsure for a moment. "I had planned to. If you still want me."

"I will always want you." That was the one thing he felt confident about. He led her to the elevator. "I'm sorry if I made you feel that I didn't."

The door to his suite closed behind them before she said, "I need a bath."

"You were wonderful tonight." He walked to the bar and took out a bottle of liquor. It was the first time in a long time. "I'm sorry I let you down."

"When?" She moved close but out of touching distance. "You defended my honor and helped in a difficult delivery. You have nothing to apologize for."

"I don't feel that way."

"Conor." This time she touched him on the arm. "Talk to me. Tell me what you were thinking back there. What upset you? For a few minutes there I didn't think you were going to help me with the colt."

"I almost didn't."

"Why? I know you're a good veterinarian, so it has to be something else."

He forced the words out. "Because it's too hard to watch a baby being born."

Confusion covered her face and she just looked at him. "I would think you'd be wonderful with babies. Of any type."

"My wife was pregnant when she killed herself."

Christina sucked in her breath. Her eyes watered. "Conor, I am so sorry." She wrapped her arms around him, pressing herself again him.

He returned her hug and pulled her against him, drawing comfort from her. They stood like that for a long time. Saying nothing and taking strength from each other. Slowly, his pain ebbed away.

"The colt brought back what had happened. Reminded me of what I had lost."

"You said nothing." She looked at him.

He cupped her cheek. "The hurt has eased since I met you. You have pulled me out of that dark place and forced me to go to work."

She smiled softly. "I did that?"

"Yes, you did." He kissed her and led her toward the bathroom. "And I intend to show you how grateful I am."

CHAPTER NINE

MONDAY MORNING, AS the sun brightened the eastern end of Churchill Downs, Christina stood at the back stretch of the racetrack. Her hands rested on the rail as she waited for the next group of horses to make their morning exercise run. Excited anticipation that came close, but wasn't quite equal to Conor's lovemaking, filled her. The exception heightened the thrill.

A warm body hers recognized immediately moved in close. She didn't have to look to know it was Conor beside her. She would miss him when he left. She didn't even want to think about it. Yet, the calendar days kept flipping by. Too soon, he would be in Ireland and she would be here. She wouldn't let herself think of him leaving.

That morning she had let him sleep and slipped out of bed. As much as she would have liked to remain with him, she wanted to make a good impression during the week of the Derby. She couldn't afford any mistakes.

Yesterday they had lounged around Conor's

luxury hotel room. They hadn't even gone out for meals. Instead, they had enjoyed room service. They had watched TV, slept and then explored each other's bodies to their hearts' content. She had never felt more desired or satisfied. That day would be treasured in her memories.

"I missed you this morning," he murmured, leaning his head close to hers.

"I had to get moving. I needed to be on time." She leaned into him.

"I know, but that doesn't mean I liked waking up without you."

Unfortunately, that would soon be something she would have to get used to. "I'm afraid it's gonna be like that most of this week."

His voice held melancholy. "I don't even want to think about it. I hate the thought of it."

"We'll just have to take it day by day."

"So what do you have on your agenda? I'm not allowed to see Gold without someone in attendance, and he has to remain in the barn stall unless he's being schooled. I'm pretty much on my own except a few hours of the day."

She looked around at all the police officers within her view. "Security is tight around here. For the horses and the rest of us. I have to admit it's more substantial than I expected."

"I'll just be checking daily with the trainer and grooms to see if there are any issues. I understand that I can't do any care. I can only confer with the track veterinarians. Still, I'll be here when he runs and will run interference if necessary. In case there's any questions about his health and care."

She grinned. "Yes, those track vets can be territorial."

"I hope one feels that way about me." His gaze met hers.

Heat floated over her skin. "This one might."

"Might?"

"Are you looking for some admiration?"

"I'll take what I can get. Mr. Guinness will be here tomorrow. I'll be picking him up from the airport and having lunch with him. Then bringing him by here in the afternoon. He will expect me to be at a meeting with the team tomorrow night."

"Looks like we both are going to be busy this week." Christina couldn't help but be disappointed she wouldn't be seeing him. She needed to get used to it.

"Do you think you will have time to show me around Churchill Downs today? I haven't even been to the stands. I would like to have a look."

"You certainly should do it before Friday or Saturday."

"You mean that all this—" he waved his hand toward the expansive grandstand on the other side of the racetrack "—all of those, will be filled?"

"That and the end fields, and the center of the track. There it's not so much about the races but mostly about the bourbon. Personally, I'd rather see the horses run."

"I would as well."

The sound of horses racing drew her attention. Loud enough that it created an anticipation in her chest. "Here they come."

The thunder of hooves came toward them, then into view as the exercise jockeys rode the horses at full capacity. They went by and into the distance as they ran into the second turn.

"When does Gold run?"

"He'll be coming around in just a few minutes."

"How does he look?" She wanted him to win for Conor.

"I'll let you be the judge."

It didn't take long before sounds of running and heavy breathing filled the air. Soon, two more horses came around the curve and before them. She grabbed Conor's forearm. "Gold looks wonderful."

"He does."

She clearly heard the pride in Conor's voice.

They watched in silence as the horses continued around the track and out of sight.

"I better get to the vets meeting." She turned to go.

He stopped her with a touch to the elbow. "Could you meet me for lunch and then show me around?"

"I'll text you when I know what my schedule will be."

"I hope I get to see you." He gave her a quick kiss on the temple.

"Me, too." She took a couple of steps and stopped again. Headed her direction was the rude man from the party on Saturday night.

"Excuse me."

Conor moved up beside her so he stood between her and the man. She stepped around him but stayed close.

The man cleared his throat. "I want to apologize. I was a jerk the other night. Bourbon loosened my tongue. I shouldn't have said what I said."

Christina didn't move. "I appreciate you coming to tell me. I hope we can work together without any problems."

"That's my intent."

She gave him a tight smile. "Mine as well."

The man looked sincere. "I heard about the colt delivery. Impressive."

"Thank you."

"Then I will see you around." His look flickered to Conor, who hadn't moved a muscle.

"I'm sure you will," Conor said in a tight voice.

The man gave them both a curt nod and left.

Christina looked at Conor. "That was nice of him."

"It would have been nicer if it hadn't happened." Conor released his fisted hands.

Her hand circled his arm. "I would like for it to be forgotten."

Conor spent the rest of his morning in the equine clinic, answering questions about Gold, then attended the track vet evaluation of the horse. Other than that, he was encouraged to leave the backside.

The rest of his week would consist of waiting and trying to catch a glimpse of Christina. Because he was associated with a horse that was racing, he was not allowed for security reasons to do any volunteer veterinary work. Which would leave him with time on his hands. He would have daily discussions with the trainer and the grooms and be at the track for any training, especially when Gold was running the Breeze or being schooled in the padlock. Other than that, he would be restricted by security.

Conor had volunteered to help out. He had seen Dr. Dillard briefly and offered to at least watch along the rail during the Breeze and at the padlock. To be a first responder. Dr. Dillard told him he would keep that in mind. Still, Conor did not anticipate being asked to help unless the man became desperate. Conor's problem was he missed being with Christina. Just the idea of not seeing her hurt.

Why had he let her matter so much? He hadn't planned on that happening. Hadn't thought it could. Despite his fear of being like his father, he had overcome it, and somehow Christina had slipped in and captured his notice. Something no one had managed to do since Louisa. He had never intended to care like this again, then came Christina.

A beep on his phone made him look. His heart jumped. Christina. She was through for the day and would meet him for lunch. She wrote she would wait for him in front of the equine clinic.

Christina greeted him with a huge smile that had him smiling like a fool back at her. It had only been a few hours since he had seen her. The woman had him acting like a love-struck teenage boy.

"I guess your morning went well." He liked seeing her so happy.

She continued to smile. "Very well. I'm going to enjoy this week."

"I'm glad to hear that." He squeezed her hand for a moment. "So where are we going for lunch?"

"There's a restaurant just off the backside. I understand from Callie they have some great burgers."

"Sounds good."

They walked down the gravel drive between the barns then crossed the road to a single-story building.

"I think you'll like this place. It's dark and has a lot of wood. It should remind you of a pub."

Something he hadn't thought of in days. Home. Interesting.

The lighting inside was dim. It took a moment for his eyes to adjust. The older building held wooden tables and chairs that had seen better days. Christina passed them up for a booth in the back. She slid in and stopped in the middle of the seat.

He waved her farther into the booth and took the space beside her. "I want to sit next to you."

"Maybe we shouldn't be so obvious."

He scanned the area. "Who here do you think cares? I certainly don't care if they know I'm attracted to you."

She grinned. "I like the idea that you are."

He took her hand and placed it on his knee.

An older man with a white apron around his waist came to take their order. They decided on hamburgers and fries.

Conor said, "Tell me how it went today."

"Really well. Not that we did anything in particular other than get orders and be reminded of how strict they are about the horses during Derby week security-wise."

"What are you going to be doing?" He rubbed the top of her hand with the pad of his thumb.

"The next two days I'll be helping with taking the daily bloodwork then watching at the padlock during schooling. The next day may be different."

"Then you're going to be everywhere."

The waiter brought their drinks.

"It sounds like it." She took a swallow.

"You'll be having some long days." He saw what little time he would have with her slipping way.

"I will. But I'm looking forward to it."

He squeezed her hand. "I'm glad this worked out for you."

"But I'll miss seeing you. Now, if Gold wins the Derby race we'll both be successful."

Conor was not sure that would make him feel successful about the trip. He already dreaded leaving her.

Their burgers came and they spent their time eating and discussing the horses that would be running.

"Are you off for the rest of the afternoon?" Conor asked.

"Yes, I can be your tour guide." She caught the drip running down her chin with a napkin.

He wished he could have licked it away. "I would like you to stay the night with me, too."

"I wish I could but I have the horses to see about." She ran her hand down his leg.

"I'll miss you."

She met his gaze. "I'll miss you, too. Are you ready to go? We'll go have a look at Churchill Downs."

"When you are."

She took out her phone and sent a text message.

"What's that about?"

"I got us a ride over to the stands. Otherwise, we would have a pretty long walk."

A few minutes later a truck pulled up in front of the restaurant.

"That's Carlos. He's one of the staff here. He said he would give us a lift." She climbed into the front passenger seat and moved over. Conor settled in beside her.

Carlos drove them back along the road they had walked earlier then veered to the left into a tunnel.

"I had no idea this was here." Conor looked around in amazement.

"Most people don't."

They came up into the sunlight on the opposite side of the track. Carlos stopped at the first gate on the grandstand they came to. Conor popped out then helped her down.

"Carlos, thanks for the ride. We'll find our own way back," Christina called over her shoulder.

He nodded and drove on.

They stood in front of the stands for a moment. "I've already told you about the twin spires, which are used as the logo for Churchill Downs. Come on, let's climb a few rows up so you can see."

Conor stood beside her, looking out at the track. "It is something. The big screens and hedges and the Winner's Circle."

"That, it is. As you can tell, we run dirt mostly here. But there is also a grass track. I understand you run mostly grass in Ireland. Both can be a mess on a rainy Derby Day."

"I can imagine. We have practiced Gold on dirt just because of this."

"The track is maintained carefully to make it as safe for the riders and horses as possible." He had seen the track groomers in action. They were a finely tuned and efficient group.

"Down there is where the starting gate is for a number of the races." She pointed to the right near the last turn. "A few races start near the first back turn. But I'm not telling you anything you don't know."

He smiled. "No, you aren't, but I enjoy hearing you talk. I love your enthusiasm."

Conor continued to listen and ask questions.

Christina was in her element and loved the race-track.

She spread her arms wide. "These stands will be overflowing on Derby Day. All to watch what they call the two greatest minutes in sports."

"I can see why they call it that." Conor couldn't help but be impressed.

"I have more to show you. Doctor Dillard made special arrangements so I can take you up to that balcony where you can see the entire track. Give you a bird's-eye view."

They went under the stands to the elevator. It took them to the sixth floor, where they stepped out into an open area with tables. She pushed through the glass doors that led to a balcony and walked all the way to the rail. "Isn't it gorgeous?"

He watched her. "It is but not as pretty as you."

Christina gave him a lopsided grin. "Thank you but you need to focus on the racetrack."

He put his hand around her waist and pulled her to his side for a little squeeze. "I'd rather concentrate on you." He let her go before she could complain. He looked at the track. "Yes, it is pretty. I still can't get over how large it is."

"It's impressive. Would you like to go see the museum?"

"There's a museum here?" He hadn't heard of it.

"Yes. It not only shows the past winners, but a short movie and history of the event."

"I would like to see it." He also wanted to make the most of the time he could have with Christina.

They returned to the elevator. The doors had hardly closed before Conor took her into his arms. His kiss had her gripping his shoulders to stand.

"I haven't had a chance to do that today and I will miss out tonight, so I'm making the most of this time alone."

The doors slid open. Christina watched him with a dazed look. He grinned. "Weren't you going to show me the museum?"

"What?" She blinked.

He chuckled. Her reaction to his kiss stroked his ego.

They walked the length of the stands and stepped out a side gate to where the museum was located. At the desk they showed their badges and entered the museum. They walked through what looked like a starting gate into the exhibit area.

Strolling along hand in hand, they circled the building, looking at the trophies, jockey outfits and discussing the famous horses that had gone on to win the Triple Crown.

"Remind me what the Triple Crown is?"

"It's when one horse wins the Kentucky Derby, the Belmont and Preakness all in the same year. That's considered the Triple Crown. Only a few horses have managed to do it. And then they go out for stud."

"Which is not a bad job if you can get it." Conor gave her a wolfish grin.

She smiled. "Every man's dream, I guess. To produce many children."

The sadness covered his face.

Her eyes turned concerned. "I'm sorry. I said that without thinking."

"It's okay."

"Would you like to have more children?" she asked softly as if unsure of his reaction.

"I don't think so. It would be too hard to lose one again."

"But you might not."

It hurt to hear her so hopeful, but he had to tell her the truth. "I couldn't take that chance."

"I think children would be worth the chance." She tugged his arm. "Let's watch this movie. That's in the round. You'll like it."

A few minutes later, they were walking out of the museum. They stopped in front of the gift shop. A number of large women's dress hats hung on a stand.

"What are the women's hats about?"

"The women wear hats on Oaks and Derby Day. Some are very extravagant. It's part of the Derby's mystique and fun."

"I'd love to see you in one."

"I'd looked pretty silly wearing one while seeing to a horse." She waved her hand up and down herself. "And one wouldn't go with my outfit."

"You deserve to experience some of the glamours of life." He would like to give that to her.

"Thank you, but I think this week is going to consist of blue jeans and boots."

He took her hand. "I guess you're right."

They returned to the track.

A golf cart approached. She waved it down. "Are you going back to the other side?"

"Yep," the woman said.

"Do you mind if we get a ride?" Christina asked.

"Hop in."

The woman dropped them off in front of the equine clinic. They walked toward her truck.

"I enjoyed my tour."

"I'm glad you did." Christina hesitated. "I guess I should get started for home."

"I wish you were staying with me. I'm sorry I can't go with you. I have to be at the airport early in the morning."

She placed her hand on his chest. "I understand." She opened the truck door.

He leaned toward her. "I want to kiss you, but I don't think this is the place for either one of us to have a public display."

Her gaze met his. "I know."

"Doesn't mean I don't want to."

"Same here." She brushed his hair back.

"Just the same, I'm going to give you a quick one." He took a step closer.

"And I'll gladly take it."

His lips brushed hers for a moment before he straightened. "I'm already missing you. I'll see you tomorrow."

"I'll make sure it happens." She offered him a small lift of her lips.

"You drive safe."

"Bye, Conor."

He watched Christina drive toward the exit. She stopped and waved out her window. She'd known he would be watching.

Christina finished taking what seemed like her hundredth blood test for the day, not to mention the number of daily records of medications that must be reviewed and overseen each day. This had to happen every day for each horse in the stables.

Now all of the competitors were securely on the backside, it had become a busy area. That would continue until Saturday evening after the last race.

She had expected such and loved the excitement of it all. It made her blood hum. Still, she was worn out each evening.

She hadn't seen Conor since she had left him the afternoon before last. She had been busy enough not to obsess over it, but when she did pause for lunch, she scanned the area, hoping for a glimpse of him. She should've anticipated it would be this way. But that didn't mean she liked it.

He was busy with Gold. Had responsibilities of his own. Mr. Guinness would expect him to focus on the race ahead. Understanding the situation didn't mean she didn't miss him. Painfully so.

Maybe it was just as well. She needed to get used to it. Soon, Conor would be gone. The problem was she had become used to him being in her life. There in the morning and again at night. Especially at night. That, she liked the best.

She had known it wouldn't last, but that didn't mean she didn't want to enjoy him while she could. Now their jobs were getting in the way. Not that either one of them could do anything about it.

That evening she drove home exhausted. She took care of the horses before going into the empty house. Where she'd found her home reassuring just weeks earlier, now she found it depressing. Lonely.

She headed for the bathroom too tired to bother with cooking a meal, not that she would have done anything more than microwave something. After a shower to wash off the dirt, sweat and manure of the day, she pulled on a shortie gown and climbed into bed.

She was almost asleep when her phone buzzed, notifying her of a text from Conor.

Come to the back door.

What was going on? She padded along the hall through the kitchen to the door. She flipped on the outside light, pushed back the curtains and found Conor standing on her stoop. She quickly unlocked the door and flung it back. "What are you doing here?"

Conor scooped her into his arms. His mouth covered hers in a deep, wet, hot kiss that shook her to the core.

Her arms went around his neck, welcoming him into her home and her heart. She missed him to the bottom of her soul. She returned his kiss, holding nothing back. Her legs wrapped his hips.

He stepped to the counter and sat her on it, then moved between her legs. His lips traveled down her cheek. He nipped the sweet skin behind her ear. "I've missed you."

"I've missed you, too. What do you mean by coming to my house in the middle of the night and kissing me senseless?" She gave him a defiant look and a teasing grin. "I'm not gonna let you in my bed."

"Honey, I think you're gonna be glad that I came to your bed."

"You have a high opinion of yourself. Do you think you can just bust into a woman's house and make demands on her?"

He studied her face. "You want me to go?"

She wrapped her arms around his neck. "Don't you dare. I've missed you."

He grinned. "Prove it."

Christina kissed him with everything she had in her. She slipped her hand between them and ran it over his tight length.

"Okay, I believe you might have missed me." He picked her up again and started down the hall.

He said between kisses, "I can't believe that I've been in the same half a mile as you for two solid days and didn't even catch a glimpse of you."

"I know what you mean." She nipped his earlobe.

He pressed his manhood against her center. "Can I stay?"

"You can if you make sure the back door is locked. I wouldn't want another man busting in."

Conor growled. "There better not be another man wanting in. I don't share." He carried her to her bed and dropped her. "I'll be right back."

She lay back and sighed. "I'll be right here waiting."

The next morning Christina woke before daylight.

Conor groaned beside her, pulling her to him. "It can't be time to get up."

"I'm afraid it is. The one thing I do hate about running a farm is always having to get up early to see about the horses every morning."

He nuzzled her neck. "You picked the wrong vocation."

"You don't say."

He kissed her cheek and rolled away from her. "You stay here, and I'll see about the horses this morning. Sleep in for a change."

She looked at him in the dim light from her clock. "Don't tease me this early in the morning. I could turn on you."

He gave her a quick kiss. "Hey, I'm not kidding. You sleep and I'll be back in a little while."

"You would do that for me?"

"Sure. Keep the bed warm." She felt the breeze when he lifted the covers.

"That, I can do. I'll owe you one." She had already turned over on her stomach.

"And I plan to collect."

"Mmm."

He kissed her bare shoulder.

Just a few weeks ago she wouldn't have trusted him enough to see to the horses.

Conor returned, crawling into bed. They made love. It was poignant, slow and sweet. None of the rushed excitement of the night before.

"Each time it becomes more difficult to leave you," he said as she climbed out of bed ahead of him.

It hurt her heart to think about him leaving. She had fallen for him hard even in the short amount of time she had known him. She couldn't imagine what the pain would be like in the future. Since she already knew there wouldn't be any tomorrows with him.

The next few days would be impossibly busy. That would be a blessing. There would be less time to think about her future without Conor. She had hoped to spend the weekend with him but instead she would be traveling back and forth from her house to Churchill Downs daily. Unfortunately, he had to remain in town those nights.

She had to break it to him sometime, that she wouldn't be staying with him. Now was as good a time as any. "I'm not gonna be able to stay with you this weekend."

"Why not?" he demanded.

"The person who I had lined up to see about the horses backed out on me. And I don't have time to call around and try to find someone else."

His happy face turned sad with his eyes downcast. "There's no one you can get?"

"Not that I know of right now."

He sat on the side of the bed looking dejected. "I hate for you to travel those extra miles when you could be closer. And with me."

"Our days have already been long and I'm sure they're gonna get longer. We wouldn't see much of each other anyway." She wouldn't be sleeping with him, either.

"That's probably true." He wouldn't look at her. "I'm tied up all day today. Tomorrow is the Oaks. Then the Derby the next." What she left out was he would be leaving after that. "As much as I hate it, I don't think we need to have any interaction anyway. Us being together might come into question since Gold stayed at my place and we know each other. I don't want there to be any questions about my integrity."

CHAPTER TEN

"INTEGRITY?" HE LOOKED at her as if she had lost her mind. "You have to be kidding."

"There can be no suspicion of impropriety."

He stood. "Then I'll drive out here."

She shook her head. "I don't think that's a good idea."

"What are you scared of?" He jerked his pants on.

"I'm scared of being accused of tampering with a horse or race. My honesty and actions could be questioned. That, I can't take a chance on."

He faced her, his legs spread in a defensive manner. "Nobody's even paying attention and that would mean not seeing me. I'm leaving soon."

"You heard that guy the other night."

"He was an idiot." Conor's voice rose.

"No, he was saying what other people are thinking."

His chin jerked up. "So you plan to go through your life worrying about that."

"I have to get used to it. This is my chance to prove myself."

Conor's brows drew together. "Who are you proving yourself to?"

"My colleagues."

He glared at her with his hands on his hips. "You are a great veterinarian. You did nothing wrong. Why do you think you need to keep telling people that?"

"Because I let them down." She found clean clothes.

"How did you do that?" His disbelief hung in the air.

"Here everyone in the horse-racing world knows everyone else or at least about them. I made them look bad."

His mouth fell open. "You didn't do it. Nelson did. You need to leave that behind and move forward. You. Were. Not. Responsible. You are a good and caring human. You have a business that is admirable. Just because your mother thought you did not measure up that does not mean that's a fact. I think you are wonderful. And enough for anyone. In fact, you are the most amazing woman I know."

"I appreciate that, but that doesn't change the fact that my name has been damaged, and I need to guard it." She headed for the bath.

He followed. "My point is it isn't about what

happened with the drugs. It's about your self-esteem."

"It doesn't do much for my self-esteem to know that you can return to Ireland so easily or that I'm not worth staying here for. You act like you really care but you don't show it."

He looked confused. "What do you mean?"

"What are you going back to? You have family but a lot of people live far away from their family. You could stay here and help run the farm with me. It doesn't seem that you're having any trouble leaving."

He followed her to the bath. "Christina, I can't make that type of commitment. I gave all I had the last time. I couldn't live through a loss like that again."

"What makes you think you would lose me? Louisa killed herself out of despair. The loss of your child was an accident. I'm not going anywhere. This is your chance to start over. To find happiness. Here with me."

He filled the doorway. "Ireland. That's my home."

"You can make your home anywhere. Even here with me."

"I can't, Christina. I can't give you what you want. A husband. Children. I just can't do it again." He glowered at her. Why couldn't he get her to understand?

"I think you could. You're just scared. Maybe it's a good thing we can't see each other for the next few days. We can say goodbye here." She turned her back on him and started the shower.

The idea hurt him more deeply that he would have anticipated. He wanted to shout no, but he just couldn't offer her what she wanted. Now was the time to walk away from her. Even if it was another form of death.

Christina wasn't sure how their conversation had turned into an ugly argument that had gone so bad so fast. Had it been from frustration over not being able to see each other? More likely, it was over the fear they wouldn't see each other again after the race. Whatever it was, she had to learn to accept it was over between her and Conor.

She'd been awake most of the night after their fight when she should've been resting. Instead, she'd spent that time going through different scenarios of how to make their situation better. She couldn't afford to have any hint of impropriety. She had learned that the hard way. Negatives were eagerly believed, while positives were harder to earn.

She worked too hard to get this opportunity to assist during the Derby week. She couldn't fail. She was sorry that Conor couldn't understand that. His reputation had not been called into question.

On Friday morning she drove onto the backside before daylight. Today would be the Oaks Race, all female horses. It would be a full day of racing. The backside was already buzzing with activity.

She had been given her assignment for the day the evening before. There were still a couple of hours before the first race. She and her partner teamed up to help with day-of blood tests. Each horse racing would have to be tested within thirty minutes of their race. This was to look for a number of medicines that could be used to enhance the horse's performance. Those were absolutely not allowed in the racing world. Horses found to have been using were immediately disqualified.

An hour before the first race she returned to the equine clinic. There she caught a golf cart along with three other veterinarians. The driver would drop them at their assigned position at the first turn of the racetrack. If there was an accident, it would only be seconds before she and her colleagues would be there to care for the horse. Other veterinarians would be doing the same along the mile-long track.

She carried medical supplies in her backpack, including different sized splints for the horses' legs, and pain medicines. Breaks and wounds were her largest concern during the actual race.

There was much more to the two days of racing than many people thought. So much took place behind the scenes. It wasn't all about running.

In the distance she could see the stands filling. For once in her life she wished she could dress more feminine, to wear something besides her T-shirt, jeans and boots. She would have liked to look less masculine and more feminine, especially today when so many other women were dressed in their finest, including a hat. Many of them would wear pink in honor of the female horses racing.

Throughout all the activity, she never saw Conor. It wasn't from the lack of trying. She searched for him wherever she went. The chances of her seeing him would be almost nothing from her station on the rail. She was in a restricted area. He would not be allowed there.

Sadness washed over her. She'd known when she stepped out of the shower the day before and Conor was gone, that it was over between them. She had to keep reminding herself of that fact. It was for the best since he would soon be returning to Ireland. At least it wouldn't be a long, drawn-out romantic drama-like parting. That, she couldn't live through.

Friday evening she drove off the backside with a tight chest filled with disappointment. She had been around hundreds of thousands of people all day, yet she felt so alone. This, she should get used to because she would carry the feeling for months and years to come.

Her phone rang. She jerked it up without looking, hoping it would be Conor. "Hello."

"I was just checking in to see how you're doing?"

"Mama. I'm fine. Busy working at Churchill Downs." She put the call in over her truck speakers.

"You got the job?"

Her mother sounded so amazed it grated on Christina's nerves. "I did."

"Even after what happened?"

"Yes, Mother. And I did nothing wrong."

"No, but you should have realized what Nelson was doing."

"We've gone over this before. I'm not up to doing it again tonight. It's been a long day."

"What're you wearing to Churchill Downs? I hope you're wearing something nice."

"The last thing I need to have on while on the ground caring for a horse that is hurt is a dress."

"But it's Churchill Downs. All the women will have dresses and hats on," her mother whined.

"Except for those who have to work like I do."

"I have never understood you and those horses." Her mother's voice carried her usual disapproving tone.

Christina sighed. Here they went again.

"Why couldn't you have done something that didn't require you to get your hands dirty?"

"Mother, I want you to stop there." Christina raised her voice. "You have spent this entire phone call making me feel like I don't measure up. My whole life, in fact. I am a good veterinarian. I have done nothing wrong, and I refuse to act like I have. I'm good enough to take care of any horse at any time, and I love what I do. If you can't talk to me in a positive way then just don't call. I'm tired and I've had a long week. I'm not going to put up with it any longer."

There was a long pause.

"Christina, I think you're overreacting."

"Mother, I'm going to say bye now. Think about what I've said before you call again." Christina hung up. For once, she felt good about herself after talking to her mother. Conor had made her feel strong enough to stand up for herself. She wanted to tell him but that wasn't going to happen.

Because of him, her life would be different. Better.

Conor struggled to act enthusiastic about the Derby Day races. It would be a long day until Gold ran. That left him with a lot of time for his mind to wander. His thoughts were more on Christina than they were on what he should be worrying about—Gold. He and Christina had broken up. Wasn't that what he wanted?

Right now, all he needed was to see her. Just a glimpse. He missed her like he never believed he would. She was so close but so far away. Was she hoping to see him as well?

Over the past few days he had remained busy but not enough so that there was no downtime. That was when thoughts of Christina filled his mind. Was she as miserable as he?

He had not slept since leaving her bed four days ago. Gold's trainer and one of the grooms had even commented on how awful he looked. It did not help that he arrived early in the day, and Mr. Guinness required him for social events in the evening. All he could think about was how much he wanted to join Christina in caring for the horses. He would even help deliver a foal if he could do that with her.

Morning after morning he had stood beside the track, hoping she would join him to watch the horses run. He was disappointed. He had missed the look of expectation that came over her face at the sound of the horses running in her direction. Along with the adrenaline rush it gave him to bring her release.

Around horses and in bed with him she was beautiful. Expressive. In her element. She loved the sights, smells and the trill of horseracing. If he wasn't careful, he would start writing odes to Thoroughbred racing and Christina. There were probably already hundreds of printed poems about the Kentucky Derby. Christina deserved just as many.

What would happen if he decided to stay in America with Christina? His entire life had been built around being true to the one you love. He had seen what it was like when a husband wasn't faithful. It slowly destroys the other person and makes the family rot from the inside out. He had been true to Louisa but now she was gone. Could he be that devoted to Christina? Rebuild his life with her?

Mr. Guinness stepped up beside him at the rail. "You have stood here each morning. At first, I thought you were that absorbed in the horses running. But then I realized you aren't looking at the horses. You're looking everywhere but at them. Who are you searching for?"

Had Conor really been that pathetic?

"Is it the woman who boarded Gold?"

"Yes." Conor continued to search the crowd.

"So what is going on between you two?"

This was not a subject the two of them normally had a conversation over. "Right now, nothing. She told me not to have anything to do with her during the races because she didn't want there to be any appearance of collusion."

"Okay, knowing the security around here I can see that. So why the long face? After Gold's race, find her."

"There's more to it than that."

"And what is that?" When Conor didn't say anything right away, he continued. "You've worked for me for years and because of that we have become friends as well. After your wife died I, along with your other friends and family, have watched you become a shell of yourself. So much so that when your brother and sister came to me and asked me if I would send you over here with Gold I agreed to mess in your life. Not something I make a habit of. We were all worried you would never return to your old self. We all wanted you to have a fresh start. A chance to get away from your memories."

"I had no idea you were in on this."

"You would never have if you hadn't looked so happy when I arrived and now you don't. I would have never said anything. But I knew our plan had worked the second I saw you. This is what we wanted for you. Not necessarily to find someone but to move on past your grief and sadness. To start living again."

"I was that bad?"

Mr. Guinness nodded. "I knew by just talking to you on the phone. Just the difference in your voice said whatever this woman had done, you needed to grab hold of it."

"Being with her would mean leaving everything I've known behind in Ireland."

"You do realize there are airplanes. You can visit. Your family can visit you. Even Gold managed to get over here." Mr. Guinness grinned. "Do I dare to tread on our friendship enough to ask how you feel about this woman?"

"I'm afraid I'm in love with her."

"That's not a bad thing, Conor."

He thought for a moment. "No, it's not. In fact, I've never felt better about myself or life in a long time."

Mr. Guinness gave Conor a slap on the shoulder. "That's what I figured. Maybe you need to give your plans some thought. See what options you can come up with. Even as miserable as you are right now, you look far better than you did before."

"Now, we should concentrate on Gold. We need to go if we're going to walk him over to the starting gate. Maybe you'll catch a glimpse of her as we go."

Conor's chest tightened. Mr. Guinness and Christina were right. There really wasn't anything left for him in Ireland that he couldn't change. His clients had slowly drifted away, and he'd let them. He was down to Gold now. Here with Christina, he could have a fresh start. They could build something together. If she would still have him.

He liked America. He liked living the lifestyle that Christina offered. So why wouldn't he stay? Because he was afraid. Of caring again and losing her, but if he didn't try then he would lose her for sure. He would have no more than he had now. Which was nothing. He knew well what nothing felt like. He didn't like it. Now he understood what it was to have Christina and he wanted that. He had to decide if it was worth stepping beyond his fear to take a hold of happiness.

Christina was worth that and more.

Christina remained in her position at the rail as the groups of owners with their families and those involved with the horses running the Derby race made their traditional walk from the barns to the starting gate.

She tried not to focus on Gold's group, but she couldn't help herself. She got a glimpse of Conor long before he reached her. Her heart fluttered hard enough she worried she might lift off. Was he as happy to see her as she was to see him? Was he still angry with her? Would he leave without telling her goodbye? The idea made her physically sick.

When the group came close enough, Conor's intent gaze locked in on hers. It didn't waver. In that moment it was only them. All the other stuff had fallen away. The thrill of seeing him buzzed through her.

Conor smiled. Concern filled his eyes but a hint of hope as well. She returned a small smile.

He didn't approach her. She appreciated him honoring her request they have no contact. Even though she longed to climb over the railing, run to him and wrap her arms around his neck to give him a kiss. She mouthed "Good luck."

His smile grew a little brighter as he continued past her on the dirt track.

Christina waited with building anticipation as each one of the horses was announced as they were put into the starting gate.

Soon, the track announcer said, "They're in the gate…and they're off!"

The horses came barreling toward her, spread out across the track. By the time they had reached her they had moved into a double line with a group in the middle.

Gold was in the group as they ran past her. She couldn't help but quietly cheer the horse and jockey on. She didn't dare be any louder.

The horses continued to run, picking up speed, and the crowd stood, hollering. From her vantage point she couldn't see even a screen to tell her how Gold was doing. She listened to the announcer as he called names and positions as the horses rounded the back turn. Seconds later the announcer said they're coming around the last curve and into the homestretch.

She heard Gold was in fourth place and the announcer then said Gold was making a move on the outside. He was in third place coming into the homestretch. The crowd was screaming louder. Gold crossed the finish line in second place.

Christina couldn't help but jump up and down. He had done so well. She was proud of the efforts of the horse, Conor and those who worked with Gold.

She wanted to run to the stands, wrap her arms around Conor and congratulate him, but she had to hold her spot. There was one more race before the day would be done.

Would Conor search her out? Or would he be celebrating?

The next forty minutes went by slowly.

She was exhausted and ready to go home by the time the races were over. She slowly made her way to her truck. Still no Conor. The horses were waiting on her. At one time she would've hoped to spend the night with Conor, telling him good-bye. Now she would be going home to an empty house and bed.

She didn't know what she had expected. They were too different. He from Ireland and she from the States. She wanted a husband and family. He a good time while he was there with no attachments. She was messy and he was tidy. He could cook and she couldn't. She wanted to live here and he had his life in Ireland. He was devoted to his dead wife and she wanted him devoted to her. They weren't meant to be.

CHAPTER ELEVEN

THE NEXT MORNING Christina crawled out of bed, fed the horses and returned to bed again. She was exhausted physically, mentally and emotionally after the past week. All she wanted now was to pull the covers over her head and stay that way for a few days, but with animals to feed and care for she couldn't.

She missed Conor with every fiber of her being. He was no doubt packed to return to Ireland. She had hoped, then prayed, he would call. The silence of her phone just added to her agitation and disappointment. She would have to learn to live without him. To be alone.

Working in the barn had been her therapy for so long and now he had ruined that. Memories of them being there hung in the air and settled in her mind. Neither reassuring nor comforting.

Tears stung her eyes. She blinked them away. Last night she had done enough of that.

A good day of rest and she would be her old self. Or at least that was the lie she kept repeating.

She brought this misery on herself. Had become too involved with Conor. Knew it while it was happening. Had told herself that and still, she walked into his arms and invited him into her bed. What had she been thinking? She hadn't been; she'd been feeling.

Rolling over, she clutched the pillow with Conor's smell still attached to her chest and buried her face in it. If she could just sleep today, then get up and start again tomorrow, maybe she could get her life back. With patience and taking care of the horses, the past three weeks would be forgotten. Then she could survive him not being there.

As much as working Derby week had meant to her, having Conor meant more. She had just realized that too late.

In the middle of the afternoon, she hauled herself out of bed. She had to get moving. She had to accept what her life looked like. Those weeks with Conor had only been a dream in the middle of reality. Now it was time to live in the latter once more. After pulling on her work clothes, she headed for the barn.

Cleaning out the stalls despite their not needing the attention would be a good distraction from her worries. She turned the music up and sang along at the top of her voice. The horses gave her a quizzical look but returned to their eating.

What was that noise? Her name? She turned.

There in the half circle of the sun coming through the large barn door stood the most wonderful sight she had ever seen. Conor. Her heartbeat roared in her ears. Her hands were sweaty and they shook. She murmured, "You're here."

"Where else should I be?" He studied her as if her answer was very important to him. "I belong here."

She staggered a moment, then planted the pitchfork into the ground to steady herself. "I thought you were leaving. That you were at least loading Gold to go home."

"No. We are both staying."

"Staying?"

Conor's mouth quirked at the corners. "As in not going."

"I know what *staying* means." She threw her shoulders back.

Conor liked this Christina the best. The one with color in her cheeks and eyes bright with determination. "Would you mind moving away from the pitchfork? It makes me a little nervous. We need to talk. I have a couple of things to ask you."

She placed the tool against one of the stall walls. "So talk."

He had hoped she might fall into his arms and welcome him back. But not his Christina. She would make him work for her. Make him bare his soul. "Gold is being put out to stud. Mr. Guinness wants me to stay here with him. In fact, I gave him the idea and volunteered for the position."

"In America?"

"Yes. In Kentucky. Mr. Guinness asked me to ask you if Gold could be stabled here. He would like me, with your assistance, to oversee the breeding program."

Christina's eyes widened and her mouth dropped, as if he was making it all up. "You would stay here? Stay in my barn?"

Conor chuckled. "Gold would stay here. I was hoping for warmer and softer accommodations."

"I...uh..."

He had never seen her this flustered.

"And where will you stay?" She looked at him.

He gave her a long, lingering look, hoping the desire he was banking did not burst into flames before they finished their discussion. "I was hoping in the house with you." His look bore into hers as he walked closer to her. "Except not in that tiny room off the kitchen."

"Then where?"

"With you."

"Is that what you want, to stay here?"

"I want to be where you are. I thought I left everything in Ireland. What I didn't know was I was coming to everything in America. You are my everything. You brought me back to life. Made me live again."

"You're willing to give up your home, your practice, your family?" She continued to watch him closely.

"I'm willing. I'll do what I must to be here with you. My life was empty and you filled it. I'll gladly do what I have to in order to have you in my life. My home was no longer home after Louisa died. I need to sell it and let somebody else create a life there. My brother and sister are there but I can visit them whenever we want. Which, by the way, I know you will like them and they will like you."

"You shouldn't have to give up everything for me."

"I see it as gaining everything. I can do what I love—caring for horses, helping you build your business and loving you the rest of my life."

She stepped back, shaking her head. "I'm not worth you giving up your entire life for."

He cupped her cheek, stopping her, and looked into her eyes. "Sweetheart, you are important enough and perfect enough just the way you are for me to flip my world. Never doubt that. You are perfect for me. The question is do you want me?"

Her gaze remained locked with his. "Of course, I want you. I've always wanted you."

"Not exactly true. I don't think you wanted me when I first showed up a few weeks ago."

She smiled. "I just wasn't ready for you then."

"And you are now?" He stepped closer.

She nodded. "Yes, because I love you."

He moved into her personal space. She smelled of something floral from her shampoo, hay and a freshness that was all her. He inhaled and savored it. "I love you, too. I never thought I would ever say those words again to a woman. Christina, you took something broken in me and put it together again. You are the glue that makes my life whole. I love you."

His lips found hers. She clung to him as if he were her lifeline.

They broke apart, breathing deeply. He maintained his hold on her. "We are going to find a good farmhand. One we can trust to see after the horses so we can sleep in, have dinner out and visit Ireland without worrying."

She looked at him with love shining in her eyes. "That sounds wonderful. By the way, I spoke to my mother the other day. She started putting me down again and I told her I wouldn't talk to her if she was going to do that. She still doesn't understand the choices I've made."

He chuckled. "I bet she won't understand you falling for an Irishman."

That look of strength filled her eyes again. "She

doesn't have to understand. All she needs to know is I love you. If she starts giving me a hard time, I'll tell her I won't let her talk to me that way. Then I will politely hang up or walk away."

"I'm proud of you. But no matter what your mother says, remember I think you are just perfect the way you are. So much so I want to marry you."

"Marry me?" Her voice squeaked with surprise.

Would she turn him down? "I love you. Why wouldn't I want to marry you?"

"Because you said you wouldn't do that again."

"That was before I knew what it was like to almost lose you. I want you beside me always."

She hesitated a moment, looked away before she said, "What about children? You know I want children."

He swallowed hard. "I cannot say that I won't be terrified of losing you or one of our children, but I can't imagine a better mother. With you at my side I can do anything. I love you and I want what you want."

She threw her arms around him and pressed her face into his chest. "I love you, too. We will have the most beautiful children. I hope they all have your accent."

"If you will take me inside to check out that soft, comfortable bed of ours I'll whisper in your ear in my accent for as long as you like." He nuzzled her neck.

She grinned. "Promise?"

"Sweetheart, I promise to do that for as long as we live. I keep my promises."

EPILOGUE

Eighteen months later

CHRISTINA WALKED ACROSS the yard toward the barn. Conor hurried out, carrying their three-month-old son, Jamie. The baby bounced in his father's arms from the pace Conor set. Wide grins covered both male faces. Jamie obviously enjoyed his father's jostling.

Even at a young age, Jamie strongly favored his father. Christina had no complaints about that. Conor was an amazing and devoted father and husband. She had never seen a man more joyous or grateful than Conor when she had told him she was pregnant. Tears had filled his eyes.

He had to work at keeping his fear at bay during the pregnancy but that had become less evident after Jamie had arrived. Now Conor seemed caught up in the enjoyment of having a child, making the most of every minute.

When her mother and father had visited for the first time, Conor had run interference between her and her mother. He often interrupted her mother when she was about to say something negative and turned the conversation toward something Christina had done recently. Apparently, her mother had gotten the message and thought before she spoke further. Conor's desire to protect her only made Christina love him more.

She looked at her husband and her son. What had she done to deserve such happiness? "What's the hurry?"

"Gold's foal is coming," Conor blurted. "Buzz is with him right now. I was coming to get you. I didn't think you'd want to miss this."

"Of course I don't." Mr. Guinness had allowed them to breed Gold with a mare that had been hurt and rehabilitated on the farm. The mare's owner had no interest in her being returned so they had agreed to keep her. Conor had fallen in love with the horse. He felt she would be a good brood mare.

They all stood outside the mare's stall. Inside, Buzz, a stable hand who had quickly turned into an invaluable employee, softly spoke to the horse. They had hired Buzz so they could have a couple of mornings a week to themselves and soon learned he could handle more responsibility. Enough so they were able to visit Ireland.

Which Christina had loved. She had fallen for it and Conor's family. They had opened their arms to her and couldn't say enough about how glad they were to see Conor happy again. She and Conor were already planning a return trip to show off Jamie at Christmastime.

The horse fidgeted, stomping her feet.

"I better check her." Conor kissed Jamie's head and handed the boy to her then turned to go.

Christina grabbed his arm while holding Jamie secure in the other. "Hey, what about me?"

Conor grinned then pulled her hard against him. His kiss was slow, deep and held promises of later. He released her and her knees wobbled. That grin returned. "I've still got it."

She whispered, "I expect to see more of it tonight."

"You let me get this foal safely into the world and we'll celebrate during Jamie's nap."

Christina giggled and swatted him on the arm. "Go on. Jamie and I'll be right over here if you need help."

Conor entered the stall. She sat in the rocker that had been a gift from Conor's brother. He had made it after Conor had told him how much she enjoyed being in the barn. Conor had positioned it in the hallway so she could be close by while nursing Jamie or for occasions such as this one.

She spent as much time in the barn as possible working around Jamie's needs. The rehabilitation business had grown, and Conor had stepped in to fill her spot there. He had also received his US license to practice. They kept a few regular patients like Mr. Owen but mostly they remained close to home.

Soon, Conor joined her. "How are things progressing?"

"It may not be as soon as I first thought." Excitement filled his voice.

Conor had high hopes for this foal. Not that they had been planning to get into racing, but he wanted to give it a try. Just to see if they could do it.

"It might be a little longer than I thought. If you want to take Jamie inside, I'll come get you." He took a seat on a bale of hay beside her.

"Nope, we are happy right here." Jamie had fallen asleep in her arms.

Conor brushed his finger down her cheek. "You know when I came here I never dreamed I could ever be this happy. I love you."

"I love you, too."

"Conor, you better come," Buzz called from the inside of the stall.

Conor popped up. "Apparently, I was wrong. It's time."

Christina moved to the stall door. She watched as Conor gently guided the gangly foal into the world.

Delight filled his voice. "We have a colt."

She continued to admire her husband as he used handfuls of hay to clean the colt off.

After washing, Conor came to stand beside her, placing an arm around her waist and bringing her next to him with Jamie between them.

Together they watched the colt sway and bob until he found his footing.

"It never gets old watching new life come into the world." Christina sighed.

"No, it doesn't. It looks like a fine colt."

"It does." She shifted Jamie.

"Let me have him." Conor took his son. "Thanks for all these moments. I don't take them for granted."

"Nor do I." She wrapped her arms around him as she watched the mare nuzzle her new baby.

"Life is good." Conor gave her a squeeze.

Christina lay her cheek on his shoulder. "That, it is."

* * * * *